Nevada Noir
Crime Nevada Style

JANICE OBERDING

CONTENTS

NEVADA NOIR   CRIME NEVADA STYLE

INTRODUCTION

Nevada is a wondrous state. Still nothing is ever all positive. And so it is the case with Nevada. There's the high cost of living, the high suicide rate which is nearly double the national rate, high opioid use, and a crime rate in Las Vegas alone that is 32% higher than the national average.

Those are statistics no state can be proud of. In spite of these drawbacks, Nevada is one of the nation's fastest growing states. It's also a tourist mecca. Over forty million passengers arrive annually at Las Vegas' McCarran International Airport. But this book is not about the state of Nevada so much as it is about crimes that have taken place within the state's boundaries. And there have been plenty.

The crimes covered here are as varied as the people involved. Some took place in the long ago time of Nevada's early days, while others are more recent like the coldhearted murder of Nevada State Controller, Kathy Augustine. Augustine was a politician with drive and ambition. She could easily have made it all the way to the Nevada Governor's mansion in Carson City...if not for her much younger husband, Chaz. Kathy Augustine's death was the ultimate betrayal. Domestic violence is real. And as much as we might want to think otherwise, it's not unheard of for one spouse to kill the other. Statistically, we are more likely to be killed by someone we know than a complete stranger. This is a sad fact. Spousal murder is a theme we see in some of the stories included in this book.

There are many things that set Nevada apart from other states. Two that play a part in crime are its 24/7 lifestyle where alcohol is readily available any hour of the day or night, and legalized prostitution. That might be alright except for the fact that illegal prostitution flourishes here as well. And although it is sometimes referred to as a *victimless crime*, the dangers of illegal prostitution are well-documented. Easy money, even if obtaining it means breaking the law and putting oneself in peril. Often women like Ruth Herman realize this too late. Fortunately, Ms. Herman's killer was brought to justice. This isn't always the case. Even with the best efforts of law enforcement a number of crimes go unsolved.

These unsolveds are always disturbing. The 1934 disappearance of Roy Frisch remains one of Reno's most baffling. Chances are we will never know what happened to Roy Frisch. Just as we may never know what became of casino employee, Bill Brennan who walked out the casino door one afternoon with $500,000 of his employer's dollars. The unsolved murder of Melvin Gordon reminds us that a killer escaped justice. He could be anybody. And that in itself is frightening. With modern forensic techniques (DNA) there is always the possibility that this person will one day be apprehended yet.

With all that cash in play at any given time, in any Nevada casino, greed is bound to surface from time to time. It's a given. Gambling is part of Nevada's colorful history. The criminal element will sometimes gamble by robbing a bank or a casino. Never mind that it tops the list of stupid-bound-to-get-caught crimes. The stories of a daring downtown Reno bank robbery and of two casino heists bear this out. Those involved in two of the three crimes were apprehended.

Are Nevada crimes really any different than those of other states?

Yes…and no. Of the millions of people who visit Nevada each year, some come to score easy money, drugs and a good time. And they don't mind breaking the law to do so. This is not to say that Nevada's population is devoid of criminals, it certainly is not. Still it's important to note that not all visitors come only to sightsee, gamble, dine and shop.

The guidebooks, with their full page colorful photographs, will tell you the multitude of wonderful things to see and do here in Nevada.

This book doesn't do that. The focus here the side of Nevada you won't find mentioned, much less discussed, in the guidebooks. This is the greedy side where ruthless mobsters once ruled Las Vegas casinos with impunity. This is the bleak side, where luck turns cold and life can change, or be lost, in the blink the eye. And that can happen anywhere. But these events happened here in the Silver State.

In a book about Nevada's crime I believe it would be remiss not to mention the mass shooting that took place in Las Vegas on October 1, 2017. And so I do. However, I have chosen not to include the massacre in this book. It is the worst mass shooting in US history; 59 people lost their lives and 851 more were injured. And while we know the identity of the person who slaughtered all those innocent people from a window at the Mirage, we don't know why he did it. And we likely never will. I have decided to leave it there knowing that someday, someone will write a comprehensive book about this terrible crime, covering every detail.

NEVADA NOIR   CRIME NEVADA STYLE

It would perhaps be nice to be alternatively the victim and the executioner...Charles Baudelaire

PART ONE
COLD BLOODED

Tupac

Young and handsome, and on the verge of a very big career, rapper/actor Tupac Shakur is the only celebrity to have been murdered in Las Vegas. September 7, 1996 was just another hot day in the desert. Except that the star studded city was teeming with more celebrities than usual.

Like Tupac, they were here for the World Boxing Association heavy weight championship fight between Bruce Seldon and Mike Tyson that was scheduled for the evening. They would be disappointed. Tyson knocked Seldon out in the first round of the fight that lasted only a minute and 49 seconds. It's one of the shortest heavyweight championship fights in boxing history.

There was probably a lot of grumbling as fight fans made their way to the exits. As Shakur and his entourage were leaving the MGM Grand Hotel they ran into gang members from Southern California and a fight ensued. Once security guards broke it up Shakur and Suge Knight went to his room for a quick change of clothes.

When he climbed into Knight's car, Shakur was not wearing his bullet proof vest. The decision to skip the vest would cost him his life.

Enroute to their party destination, Club 662, they cruised along with the sun roof open and the music booming. They were young and enjoying themselves. Ten minutes into the journey Suge Knight pulled up to a redlight at the corner of Flamingo and Koval Lane. A white Cadillac pulled up beside them. Its occupants rolled down their windows and opened fire. Shakur was struck four times.

He died at the University Medical Center of Southern Nevada a week later without ever having gained consciousness. Police have speculated who was involved in the murder of Tupac Shakur, it remains unsolved.

Nevada's Highway of Mystery 1-80

Nevada's Highway 50 is known the world over as the Loneliest Road in America. It is indeed that. It's possible to drive Highway 50 for long stretches without encountering another vehicle. The more heavily traveled Highway 80, which some call the *Big Lonely* also cuts across the vast Northern Nevada desert, and is noteworthy for a very different reason. Since 1978 three people have mysteriously vanished out here in Nevada's desert while traveling along I-80. Only their automobiles, in perfect working order, were left behind.

Numerous Jane Doe bodies have been dumped along this same stretch of highway. Their murders, like their identities, are unsolved. Some believe that a trucker serial killer is at work on this highway that connects California, Nevada and Utah. Is a serial killer responsible for the deaths and disappearances along this highway?

October 27, 1978. Two days after the low budget, high grossing slasher/horror film, *Halloween* was released to theaters, a horrifying discovery was made near Imlay (along i-80) when a shallow grave was discovered just off Scossa Road. The grave contained the skeletal remains of a woman tucked into a travel bag. It was determined that she was approximately 40-50 years old and had been dead six months.

In 2009 the FBI announced its Highway Serial Killings initiative (HSK) that would assist local law enforcement with such cases. The FBI noted that the victims were primarily women and the suspects were predominately long haul truckers. From 1979 to 2009 more than five hundred bodies were dumped along the nation's highways. Since the inception of HSK ten suspects have been arrested.

I can't help but wonder if truck driving serial killers have anything to do with the following three disappearances.

Seventy-three year old grandmother Nan Dixon set out alone on September 21, 1978 from Grass Valley California in her lime green 1976 Datsun B210. Her plan was to visit her brother in the ghost town of Seven Troughs Nevada about 210 miles east on I-80. She never arrived.

Searches were conducted but there was no sign of the woman or her car. Three months after his wife's disappearance Mr. Dixon noticed that $4.18 had been spent on their credit card for gas at a gas station in Lovelock, approximately 30 miles from Seven Troughs. On Thanksgiving Day 1982 Nan Dixon's car was discovered by hunters in an area that had previously been searched by ground and air. A short distance from the Seven Troughs turnoff, the car looked as if it had deliberately been driven down to the ravine.

Stephanie Kelly Stroh took a year off college and was hitchhiking across the country. On October 15, 1987 the 21 year old stopped in Wells at the Four Way Café and Truck Stop at the junction of Highway 93 and i-80 to call her parents in San Francisco to tell them not to worry she had a ride and was coming home. They never heard from her again.

Convicted serial killer, Tommy Lynn Sells confessed to Ms. Stroh's murder with a lurid story. According to Sells, they took LSD together then he strangled her, and encased her body in cement before dumping it into a hot springs. Investigators did not believe this confession. Sells was executed in Texas on April 3, 2014 for another murder.

On Valentine's Day 2006 62 year old Judy Casida wrote a note to her husband and left Reno driving her white 1991 Mazda truck. She was last seen at the McDonalds in Lovelock about 93 miles east of Reno. Her truck was found three days later at the desolate Pumpernickel Valley Exit 205 near the town of Winnemucca, which is about 166 miles east of Reno on I-80. There was no sign of Ms. Casida.

MISSING

IF YOU HAVE INFORMATION ABOUT PATRICK F. CARNES
CALL 775-623-6429 OR JIM CARNES 775-846-2712

PATRICK F. CARNES
AND DOG LUCKY

Missing From: RENO
Date Missing: APRIL 14, 2011
Date of Birth: JAN. 30, 1925
Age: 86
Sex: Male
Height: 5'11"
Weight: 180
Build: Thin
Eyes: BLUE
Hair: BALD/GREY
Race: Caucasian
Complexion: Fair

Clothing: UNKNOWN

PATRICK WEARS GLASSES
FULLTIME AND NEVER GOES
ANYWHERE WITHOUT LUCKY

CIRCUMSTANCES

PATRICK WAS DRIVING WITH HIS
LIFELONG COMPANION LUCKY,
TRAVELING WEST ON INTERSTATE
FROM OHIO TO RENO. HIS VEHICLE
WAS FOUND IN GOOD CONDITION
20 MILES EAST OF WINNEMUCCA
ON THURSDAY, APRIL 14 2011.

PATRICK F. CARNES AND HIS LIFELONG COMPANION LUCKY

Five years later Patrick Carnes was headed home to Reno from a visit with family in Ohio. The 86 year old World War II vet's only traveling companion was his beloved dog Lucky.

A Nevada Highway Patrolman stopped Carnes near Wells for his failure to change lanes when coming upon the officer involved in a traffic stop.

The elderly man was tired. He told the officer that he would never drive at night again then added, "I am only following him because he is going to Elko."

Who was he following? And why? Had he somehow put his trust in the wrong person, or persons? It did seem as if he was traveling close behind a big rig. The officer glanced in the back seat to see Lucky happily wagging his tail, and let Carnes off with a warning. This was the last time anyone would ever see Patrick Carnes or Lucky.

Early the next morning a mine employee was on her way to work when she spotted Carnes' dark green Subaru Forrester at Pumpernickel Valley Exit 205.

Thinking it an odd place to be parked, she called the Humboldt Sheriff Department and reported it.

There is the possibility that Carnes let Lucky out of the car to relieve himself and the dog wandered off. While searching for his dog Carnes may have become disoriented in the darkness and died. I had wondered about this possibility. And when I recently spoke with his son James, I asked.

"Lucky was a very obedient dog." He told me.

"So he wouldn't have just run off?" I asked.

"No." He told me.

Patrick Carnes' vehicle and that of Judith Casida was discovered off the same exit. This seems to point to something more sinister than someone simply getting out of their vehicle and becoming disoriented. Both vehicles had plenty of gas and appeared to have been dumped at this location.

Hopefully one day someone will come forward with the answers and give these families closure that will end the anguish of not knowing what became of their loved one.

Just a Kid

Prostitution is illegal in Las Vegas. That and forty bucks will get you a buffet meal at some of the high class hotshot hotel casinos in town. But it doesn't do a thing to stop prostitution in Vegas. Once someone sees all that quick and easy money to be made, falling into lockstep in a pair of stilettos gets a whole lot easier, especially when a good looking, glib tongued pimp is delivering a seductive line about love and romance. Young women fall for it every day...and every night. It's not your parents' love story.

In July 1997 she ran away from home. She wasn't a woman, wasn't even old enough to vote, or drink, or catch some of the topless revues on the strip. She was just a teenage runaway who came to Las Vegas, looking for money and excitement, like thousands of other teens do every year. At sixteen she was wise beyond her years. She'd come here from Northern California. A California girl smart enough to know she needed to pose as an adult to play in this game.

So she went to Arizona, where she presented a fake birth certificate, applied for, and received, a driver's license that gave her age as 21. With her make-up and her hair styled, she looked older than sixteen. She had a legit license. And so she became a *legal* adult. Alana Alvarado, a pretty woman living it up in Las Vegas. Quaffing cocktails in hotel/casinos dimly lit bars, she scoped out potential customers. *This one looked nice, that one didn't, this one had money to spend, that one had less bills in his wallet than she did. Credit cards didn't count.*

As Alana, she raked in the money. She worked most of the big name places, until someone got wise (they always do) and reported her to security. And out on her ass, she went. It didn't deter her. Neither did the thirteen prostitution citations she'd been issued in her short time in Vegas. She paid her attorney very well, stayed out of jail, and kept on being Alana Alvarado, prostitute. In October, she was back at the Luxor and looking for business. At the bar she met Michael Joseph Hathaway, also from Northern California. After some talk, Hathaway agreed to pay *Alana* $300 for a blow job. And up to his room they went.

Once behind closed doors and the deal done, Hathaway wanted more. How much for intercourse, he asked. *Alana* thought quickly. That would cost him more, much more. Fifteen hundred dollars was her price. And she told him so. This wasn't what Hathaway wanted to hear. He grabbed *Alana* around the neck and started choking her. She begged him not kill her. He released his hands and let her fall to the floor. She was still breathing, but barely. Hathaway finished her off by standing on her windpipe for several minutes, until he was certain she was dead. Then he sexually assaulted her.

He left *Alana* there in his room at the Luxor, where a hotel maid discovered her body the next morning. Alana Alvarado, only she wasn't. Her name was Sara Gruber and she was just a kid. A kid who believed when a pimp promised her love, good-times and lotsa money; a kid who fell in with a pimp who drove her to Las Vegas where she worked the streets for him until she met a killer...

In 1998 Michael Joseph Hathaway confessed to killing Sara Gruber. He was sentenced to 20 years for the crime.

Senseless

Like 1950s Charles Starkweather and Caril Ann Fugate and 1930s Bonnie and Clyde, Jerad and Amanda Miller formed a coldblooded killing duo. Starkweather and Fugate were thrill killers, Bonnie and Clyde robbed banks, the Millers were angry with the government and authority.

Shortly before noon on June 8, 2014, Las Vegas Police officers Igor Soldo and Alyn Beck sat down to eat their lunch at a pizza restaurant. The Millers approached them and without warning Jerad Miller shot Soldo in the back of the head then turned and shot Beck in the throat.

When the downed officer tried desperately to draw his weapon, both Millers opened fire on him. They then covered the bodies with a yellow *Don't Tread on Me* flag and a swastika. A hastily scribbled note that read, *this is the beginning of the revolution* was also left with the bodies.

The two killers then ran to a nearby Walmart. Yelling at customers to leave the store, they took up positions in the rear of the building. Amanda shot and killed an armed man who'd tried to stop Jared.

Police swarmed the building. And a gun battle quickly ensued. Like Bonnie and Clyde, Jared and Amanda Miller went down in a hail of bullets. Jared died first.

When she realized the hopelessness of her situation, the injured Amanda put a gun to her head and pulled the trigger.

The Clark County District Attorney Report on Use of Force Legal Analysis Surrounding Legal Analysis Surrounding the Deaths of Jerad and Amanda Miller on June 8, 2014, states that the *incident* in Walmart lasted 24 minutes. During this time, the Millers fired 29 shots and the police officers only 16. Toxicology report indicated that Jared had Marijuana in his blood. Amanda did not.

Five lives (including those of the two killers,) senselessly lost on a hot summer day in June. Just what set it all in motion, we'll never know.

Seeing Red

Thousands of conventions are held each year in Las Vegas. James Flansburg was attending one. After the speeches, sales pitches and backslapping he wandered into one of the bars at the Mandalay Bay, where he was staying. There he met twenty-something Bridget Gray. It was March 3rd, Bridget's birthday and she was working. If he wanted a good time, she could provide it, for a fee.

Flansburg was alone. Why not? And up to his room on the 25th floor they went. Worse luck; when they arrived in his room, he discovered his shortage of cash. Isn't that why the ATM was invented? It was. After a quick trip to the ATM, he was flush with cash. A price was agreed upon and Bridget was paid.

He went into the bathroom and she quickly slipped out of her clothing. His slacks were neatly folded across a chair. Curiosity got the better of Bridget. With her back to the bathroom door, she rifled through his pants pockets. Opening his wallet, she pulled out a few bills. When he came out of the bathroom and saw what she was doing, he was furious. How dare this woman steal from him?

Before Bridget could say *sorry* he pounced on her and strangled her to death. Now Flansburg had a problem. What to do with a very dead woman in one's room on the 25th floor? He flushed her dress down the toilet, and stuffed her stilettos and sweater in the box springs of the mattress. Then he pulled her body out into the hallway and gently closed the door. Out of sight, out of mind; until the police came calling with questions.

Like the three monkeys, he saw nothing, he heard nothing and he was saying nothing. While police checked clues, Flansburg beat it back to Santa Ana, California and tried to forget. Nothing doing. A check of surveillance video showed James Flansburg and Bridget Gray walking together in the hallway and the casino and at the ATM. In May 2009 he confessed to the murder and was sentenced to ten years in the Nevada state prison.

The Death of Willebaldo Dorantes Antonio

They didn't know where their romance might take them. But they were willing to take the chance. Willebaldo Dorantes Antonio and Caren Chali had been losers in love before and were willing to gamble that their relationship would turn out better than those previous.

As undocumented immigrants they knew about taking chances. They minded their own business, kept their heads down and worked at the hotdog stand inside the Luxor. The one problem was Omar Rueda Denvers, Caren's former boyfriend and father of her child. Omar had dumped her once... now he wanted her back. But Caren had moved on. She was happy with Willebaldo, and told Omar so.

At four in the morning, May 7, 2007 Caren and Willebaldo finished their eight hour shift and walked to his car in the Luxor parking garage. As they neared his 1995 Dodge they noticed that someone had placed a Styrofoam coffee cup on the car's hood.

"Get in the car." Willebaldo told her.

Caren reach for the door handle idly watching as Willebaldo lifted the cup...suddenly, the deafening boom.

Later Chali would testify for the prosecution in the case of Omar Rueda Denvers.

Speaking through an interpreter, she said. "I turned around to Willebaldo was...he wasn't there anymore. I ran around the car...I only remember that he didn't have his fingers."

Within four days of Willebaldo Dorantes Antonio's death, the police would arrest Omar Rueda Denvers and Porfirio Duarte Herrera, the man who had made the bomb for him.

During opening statements the prosecutor said of the bomb, "It was an extremely powerful bomb. It was by its design and how it was structured to detonate designed for one sole purpose and that was to kill."

In describing Willebaldo Dorantes Antonio's injuries Luxor security guard Scott Casey testified, "He was laying on his side. He had a pool of blood around his head. His right hand was gone. Skin was hanging off of his knuckles. He kind of moaned and shrugged."

Both Denvers and Duarte-Herrera were found guilty of murder and sentenced to live in prison without the possibility of parole.

Caren Chali and her child were deported.

Ruth

They are not afraid. And the legalities of their chosen profession are not a deterrent to the young women who openly ply their trade on the streets of Reno and Las Vegas. This keeps police officers in both cities busy trying to cope with the myriad of problems associated with illegal prostitution: drugs, robbery, rape, assault, and an occasional murder. Getting into the business is almost too easy. A hard working woman, who manages to stay clear of vice-officers, can earn more in one night than the average casino worker does in a week. It's a simple matter of economics; money is what it's all about.

Wednesday, January 5, 1994. The thousands of holiday revelers who had crammed into downtown Reno to welcome in the New Year were long gone. Nothing much going on, the streets were nearly deserted. A bone chilling wind whipped across the city, sending most of the women who regularly worked Fourth Street, scurrying back to the warmth of their hotel rooms. Ruth Herman wasn't to be so lucky.

The 31 year old prostitute couldn't afford to call it a night. Ever in need of cash, she trudged a lonely path up and down her block of Fourth. Once in a while she glanced across the street at her boyfriend. One nod from him, and she too would retreat to the sparse comfort of a shabby hotel room. In vain, she waited for that okay. She stopped in front of a bar and lit a cigarette. As she stood shivering and watching smoke spiral up into the wind a dark blue truck pulled up to the curb.

From his vantage point cross the street, Ruth's boyfriend watched as she leaned into the passenger window and talked with the truck's driver. That's someone else, maybe a friend...not a trick, he thought. No money there; time's wasting...why doesn't she get back to work, he wondered. Before he had time to think it over, she opened the door and climbed into the truck. A trick after all...he watched as the truck made a U turn and sped down Fourth, not realizing it would be the last time he saw Ruth alive.

Early Thursday morning a man was enjoying an early morning jog along the Truckee River in Mayberry Park, an industrial area west of the Reno City limits. Something in the water caught his eye. Curious, he crept closer. The partially clothed body of a woman was floating in the Truckee's icy water. The shaken man notified authorities and the normally quiet park buzzed with activity. Washoe County Sheriff's deputies quickly cordoned the area off while a search was conducted for the victim's missing clothing and identification; none were found. Positioning of the body, bruising around the neck and drag marks that led from a sandy section of the park down to the river's edge, were clear indicators that detectives were faced with the Reno area's first homicide of the New Year.

The body was photographed from every angle, carefully pulled from the water and transported to the coroner's office. Whatever secrets this victim was taking to her grave, the manner of her death, would not be among them. An autopsy was scheduled for that afternoon.

News of the discovery in Mayberry Park was released to the public and the Reno Police Department was swamped with phone calls. One frantic caller was more persistent than the others; he insisted that he be put through immediately to the person in charge of the case.

With the lead investigator on the phone, the caller started to tell an odd story. His roommate was a prostitute who turned tricks in Mayberry Park. She hadn't returned home and he was concerned. The investigator asked a straightforward question.

"Did your roommate have any scars or distinguishing marks?"

Without hesitation the caller said, "Yes! She's got this scar across her stomach." The investigator had noticed the purple scar on the woman's body when they pulled it from the water. Now, he knew, unofficially at least, who the victim was, and why she had been in the park on such a cold night. Subsequent fingerprints and photographs faxed from law enforcement in Ohio would confirm the dead woman's identity as that of Ruth Herman.

As do most people in his line of work, Ruth's boyfriend/pimp wanted as little as possible to do with the law. Like it or not, her murder placed him squarely in the middle of a homicide investigation. Anxious to cooperate, he described the truck he watched Ruth get in. The truck's driver was a young blonde man and yes, he reluctantly agreed to accompany officers on a drive through the city to point out similar vehicles.

Ruth was gone. He reasoned that the sooner the police had her killer, the sooner they would leave him alone.

Meanwhile out in Mayberry Park, investigators continued to work through the night. One man would later testify, "We actually went swimming that night. It was really uncomfortable. We did a downstream search and we did an upstream search. We walked through bushes and down paths..."

Two key pieces of evidence were discovered in the search, an empty beer bottle and a sales receipt from the Woolworth's store in Park Lane Mall. The receipt was dated 1-5-94 and bore an employee I.D. number.

The mood and Fourth Street was somber. Until Ruth's killer was apprehended the women who worked this street would look at every stranger with more suspicion than usual. Detectives questioned known prostitutes. Surely one of them knew something that might help. None of the women could remember having tricked with the blonde man, or seeing him with Ruth Herman on the night of her murder.

This wasn't television in which the killer is apprehended within the constraints of an hour long show. No one in Ruth's line of work had any useful information. Luckily an undercover police officer did. He remembered a woman with an interesting story to tell. And with any luck, she might be able to help them identify their killer.

The detectives found the pretty young prostitute drinking alone in one of the downtown bars. To their surprised she was cooperative and eager to help. She sipped her drink, and told them about an unpleasant experience with a customer three months earlier.

"He wanted to take me to Mayberry Park, but I told him no. I don't go off my beat because it's...it's dangerous to go off your street. I told him we could go behind a building, or get a room. But he didn't want to. So I agreed to go to his house in Sun Valley."

The investigators ears perked up as she continued to talk, "we drank a couple of beers at his place, and then I asked him to pay me before we...before we had sex. That made him mad. Before I knew what was happening, he had his hands around my neck and was choking me unconscious. "

"Did you report this incident to the police?" One of the investigators asked.

"I told the undercover and the black and white about him…. No one seemed to care, until now."

With her description of the attacker, and of his dark colored truck, the detectives realized they were on to something.

She wanted to see this man behind bars. When asked, she readily agreed to accompany them as they drove around Sun Valley in search of the home she'd been attacked in.

They'd driven around Sun Valley for nearly an hour when she suddenly pointed to a mobile home and said, "That's it! That's the place."

A surveillance team was placed at the scene.

Three days after Ruth Herman's murder, surveillance observed the suspect thoroughly cleaning the interior of his truck. They were set to close in on him. When he and his girlfriend left the home and headed toward Reno, detectives followed closely. At the first redlight, they stopped the truck and asked him to accompany them to the Sheriff's department.

Telling his girlfriend not to worry, that he'd see her later, the suspect calmly got into the back of the officers' car. On the drive to the Sheriff's department he seemed friendly and composed. Once they arrived at their destination he was suddenly fidgety. He changed his story several times and denied driving the truck on the night of the murder. It belonged to his girlfriend, and he didn't even have a valid driver's license.

Finally he admitted he'd been driving the vehicle on the night of January 5th but had not gone to Mayberry Park. He told them he'd been with a prostitute on the night in question, but denied any knowledge of her death.

They were certain they had their man. A seizure order was obtained by the District Attorney's office and blood and hair samples were taken from him.

During the collection of the samples he asked to finish his interview. After being re-Mirandized, he confessed to killing Ruth Herman, claiming it had been self-defense.

"She came at me with a knife," He said. Then, calmly crushing out his cigarette, he admitted there had been no knife.

According to her killer, going to Mayberry Park had been Ruth's idea. She lived in one of the nearby hotels on West Fourth and thought the park was out of the jurisdiction of the Reno PD vice squad. It was a cheap and private place to turn a trick because it was usually deserted by nightfall.

He told them that they got to the park and Ruth quickly removed her blue jeans, black leather jacket, and the expensive sport shoes he'd given her months earlier. It was cold in the truck so they drank a few beers and talked to warm up some. She was still cold. But he was tired of waiting and wanted to have sex.

That's when they realized that neither of them had a condom. He didn't mind, but she did. She kept shoving him away; he kept insisting. Then she pushed him away and said something she shouldn't have. She told him that she was afraid she might have AIDS. Her words enraged him. He grabbed her around her neck and his grip, he explained,

"...kept getting tighter and tighter..I couldn't let go. I just kept doing it...."

When he realized that she was dead, he dragged her body from the truck to the river and dumped it in. He explained the sales slip from Woolworths. His girlfriend worked there. And on the day of the murder he'd gone to the store and asked her to buy him some things with her employee discount. He'd crumpled the sale receipt and thrown it in the truck; it must have fallen out when he pulled the dead woman from the truck.

Matter of factly he told investigators, "I kept her lighter and her two dollars." Officers would later find the lighter hidden in a kitchen cabinet at his girlfriend's home.

Kelly Dean Mickelson stood trial for the murder of Ruth Herman on May 31, 1994. The forensic pathologist who performed the autopsy on Ms. Herman testified,

"In addition to the gross and initial autopsy examination, I collected fluids and tissue which have been submitted for toxicology examination. I did the initial drug screen on urine which demonstrated cocaine, or cocaine metabolites present within the urine."

Further tests would prove that Ms. Herman did not have AIDS.

Among the prosecutor's witnesses were three women who testified to the physical abuse that had been inflicted upon them by the defendant. One of them told the court that Mickelson had raped her when she was just fourteen years old. After a short deliberation, the jury found twenty-nine year old, Kelly Dean Mickelson guilty.

Calling him "a deadly menace to the community" Judge Deborah Agosti sentenced him to life without the possibility of parole.

Out in the Desert

According to a long told Vegas tale, the desert outside Las Vegas holds a lot of secrets...and just as many bodies. It's the perfect spot for a body dump. Some are never discovered. The coyotes see to that. Those that are found may never be identified. The body of Al Bramlet fit neither category.

February 24, 1977 President of Culinary Union Al Bramlet was returning from a union business trip to Reno when he vanished from McCarran International Airport. Bramlet who had virtually closed down the strip with a strike a year earlier was popular with union members. He treated those who worked their asses off in the casino service industry with respect, a respect that management often withheld. Al could talk the talk. He was one of them, although he wore more expensive clothes and jewelry, drove a nicer car and lived in a higher class neighborhood than most of them ever would. This was thanks to his mob connections.

He might have politely asked his server to refill his coffee cup, and left a generous toke when he finished his meal, but not everyone liked Al. He had some powerful enemies. In its March 14, 1977 issue *Time Magazine* said Bramlet...*made enemies as easily as gamblers throw dice.*

The sharp dressing sixty year old Bramlet's worried wife of two months contacted the FBI to help in locating her husband. The 22,000 Culinary Union also wanted answers. Bramlet's assistant Ben Schmoutey announced a $25,000 reward for information on his whereabouts. Bramlet after all, was well liked by the men and women of the union

On March 17ᵗʰ St. Patrick's Day they found Bramlet. His bullet ridden nude body was discovered by rock hounds in a shallow grave in the desert southwest of Las Vegas.

Bramlet had been shot in the head. He had brought too much attention to himself and thus caused problems for the underworld and its involvement in the union. Al Bramlet had to be taken care of.

An informant who had intimate knowledge of the murder had already come forward. Eugene Vaughn told a sad sordid story. He was with the two killers when they picked up Bramlet at the airport and drove him to the desert and after offering him a drink of whiskey, shot and killed him. Investigators were not surprised to learn that the father/son hitman team of Tom and Gramby Hanley was responsible.

With a witness and a strong case, it didn't take prosecutors long to convict the Hanleys. Tom Hanley died before ever seeing the inside of a prison cell. Gramby Hanley remains incarcerated.

.

Honeymoon Horror

This senseless crime is one for the wrong place wrong time category. August 23, 1962 was Jack Foster's 23ʳᵈ birthday. This year there would be no celebrations. The young bartender clung to life in the Intensive Care Unit at the Washoe County Hospital in Reno. Before the day was out, he would die, and 19 year old Lester Morford III would be arraigned for his murder...

Morford came to Reno from Santa Rosa California. Too young for gambling, the itinerant ranch hand wandered the city's downtown streets taking in the nightlife from the outside looking in. He wanted to get high. So he purchased several tubes of airplane glue, some sodas and candy bars, and settled in at a Center Street motel that didn't cost too much.

Jack and Patricia drove to Reno from Oregon with plans to start their new life together. They would be married, celebrate Jack's birthday, and then head back home. On a tight budget, they chose a clean, but reasonably priced motel. Maybe next year they could afford a fancier room.

A brief wedding chapel ceremony and they were man and wife. The name Patricia Foster still sounded strange to the new bride, but she had a lifetime to get used to it. Giddy and in love, the Fosters had no inkling of just how short the time between "till death do you part" and that parting would be. They couldn't have known that their motel room was just two doors away from that of a monster.

And he watched them. He sniffed airplane glue and he waited and he sniffed more glue. Then he purchased a gun at the local pawnshop; now he was set to pounce.

Early in the morning, while most of the motel's guests still slept, someone pounded roughly on the newlyweds' room door. Jack opened the door with a smile on his face. The maid would have to come back later, and he was set to tell her so. Instead of the middle-age woman he expected, a young man glared angrily at him.

In an instant, the man thrust his full weight against the door and was standing in their room. Brandishing his new gun, he ordered the Fosters to lie face down on the floor. They did as they were told, and he hurriedly tore strips from the pillowcases. After tying their hands behind their backs, he yanked them to their feet. Pulling the curtains back, he scanned the parking lot. Satisfied that no one was around, he untied their hands with a warning to Jack "You try anything funny and I'll shoot your lady. Now quick, let's all get in your car, we're all goin' for a ride."

Inside the car he tied Jack's hands to the steering wheel and said, "Drive toward home. I'll give you directions."

His hands tied to the steering wheel, Foster drove as he was directed, west on Highway 40 up toward Truckee and on toward Lake Tahoe. Under any other circumstances, Patricia might have enjoyed the scenery before them, now she could only cower in the front seat wondering just what this crazy man planned on doing with her and her new husband.

They drove in a silence broken only by their captor's directions; daylight slowly gave way to darkness. "You think I'm some kinda bum?" Morton finally asked. "Well, I'm not. Here, here's some gas money." He flung a dollar bill at Jack who silently guided the car along the narrow highway. As the car passed the casinos, she thought of the casino they'd been in the night before. Now,

Patricia held back tears and stared at the lights that sparkled on Lake Tahoe. Why was he doing this to them? Would this nightmare ever end?

When the car neared the summit on Mt. Rose Highway, Morford ordered Jack to pull to the side of the road.

"Wanna smoke?" He asked. The Fosters nodded eagerly. It had been hours since either of them had had a cigarette. He lit two cigarettes and passed one to Patricia.

"Share yours with him."

Her hands trembled as she held the cigarette for her husband to take a few deep draws. Jack managed a slight smile of thanks, and she put the cigarette to her lips. While they sat smoking in the car, Morford stared intently at Foster. Suddenly he pulled his gun, reached across Patricia and shot him in the forehead. She screamed in horror, grabbing for her husband.

"Shut up! Shut up or I'll kill you too!"

There was no stopping the tears now.

"Get in the backseat! You're mine now."

Patricia did as she was told. After raping her, Morford made her watch as he pulled her husband's body from the car and pushed it over an embankment. Then he grabbed the terrified woman by the arms and shoved her back in the car. As the car raced down the treacherous Mount Rose Highway toward Carson City, she sobbed loudly. There had to be a way to escape from this madman.

At the bottom of the hill he pulled the car to the side of the road and raped her once again. Patricia focused on escape. If she wanted to survive, she would have to run from this animal as soon as she could; her opportunity came as Morton sped through Carson City. Patricia opened the passenger door and jumped out onto the pavement. Stumbling to her feet, she started to run. Morton didn't look back. The ordeal was over. Later, when asked why he had shot Jack Foster, Morton said. "I just leaned over and shot him… I just got the notion."

There would be no sensational trial; Morford plead guilty. His fate would be decided by a panel of three judges.

He would be given a death sentence.

The Supreme Court's decision in *Furman v. Georgia, 408 U.S. 153 (1972)* effectively abolished the death penalty of those inmates who waited on Death Row. Morford was given life without; he died at the Nevada State prison in Carson City several years ago.

Palomino Club

There's an old saying that lightning never strikes twice in the same place. This isn't true when it comes to murder. The Palomino Club is a North Las Vegas landmark. It is also the only strip club in Vegas that offers alcohol and entertainment that includes nude dancers. There's a reason for this. The Palomino was opened in 1969 by Paul Perry and was thus *grandfathered in* before such restrictions were placed on strip clubs. But nothing lasts forever, and that license is set to expire in 2019. In 2000 Perry's son Jack was co-managing the club along with Kenneth Rowan. It was a good arrangement until the morning of December 27, 2000. That's when Jack Perry shot and killed Kenneth Rowan at the Palomino. While Perry readily admitted to the killing he would not give a reason. It was thought that an argument between the two men over Perry's belief that Rowan was trying to buy the club and shut him out was the impetus   Ed Kane, Chief Deputy District Attorney Clark County was perplexed and admitted we may never know all the details of the murder. In court, Perry apologized to both families and claimed to be remorseful. He then made a deal and pled guilty. He was sentenced to life with the possibility of parole in ten years.   In 2003 Luis Hidalgo Jr. took over the club. Along with his son Luis Hidalgo III and his girlfriend Anabel Espindola he made some changes. One of them was an all-male nude act known as the Palomino Stallions. This, he reasoned, would bring in more female customers. Two years later, the booze was still flowing and the nude dancers were still strutting their stuff. And forty-four year old Timothy TJ Hadland went to work at the club as the night doorman. He saw it as a great side gig that supplemented his income and helped with the expense of raising teenagers.

In early May 2005 Hadland quit his job amidst bitter feelings. He didn't go quietly, and had some unflattering things to say about the club and its owners. Management at the Palomino, he said, was being unfair to the competition by diverting customers away from their establishments. In order to do this they were paying cabdrivers hefty fees to bring customers to the Palomino.

This cost the Palomino. And it infuriated the Hidalgos and Espindola when they heard about it. These were not the sort of people who sat down and discussed their differences. Two weeks after he quit the Palomino Club, TJ Hadland's body was discovered on a lonely road near Lake Mead.

He'd driven there to meet his friend and former co-worker Deangelo Carroll. Weed, he'd come for weed. While Hadland came alone in the darkness, Carroll had not. He had three others in the Palomino Club van with him. One of them slipped out of the van and shot TJ Hadland in the head as he stood talking to Carroll at the drivers open window.

They'd carried out the $5000 contract. Leaving TJ Hadland's lifeless body with Palomino Club ads scattered around it, Carroll spun the van around and headed back to Las Vegas.

In their haste to get away from the scene, none of the four men thought to check Hadland's cell phone which was left on the front seat of his car. Care to guess who was his last phone call? Deangelo Carroll of course; and it didn't take long for investigators to come knocking at his door.

Criminals tend to turn on each other like cannibals when the heat is on. Deangelo Carroll, Anabel Espindola and Kenneth Counts were true to form. They sought deals in exchange for *talking*. The Hidalgos hired Dominic Gentile, one of Las Vegas' top attorneys and prepared to fight the charges against them. Attorney fees are steep. In order to pay Gentile the Hidalgos sold the Palomino to him in exchange for legal services.

In 2007 two years after the murder of Timothy Hadland, Luis Hidalgo Jr. and Luis Hidalgo 111 were each sentenced to 20 years to life imprisonment with the possibility of parole. They would unsuccessfully appeal the sentence in 2012. In exchange for her guilty plea of voluntary manslaughter with a deadly weapon and her testimony, Anabel Espindola was released for time served. Deangelo Carroll was sentenced to life imprisonment with the possibility of parole. Kenneth Counts, the actual shooter was convicted of conspiracy to commit murder and sentenced to an 8 to 20 year sentence.

Dominic Gentile sold the Palomino Club to his son Adam, who still operates it.

The Snake Lady Murder

It was the cat. On February 20, 1976, the distressed feline was yowling so that an anonymous call was made to the Reno Police Department telling them to check an apartment at 150 Ralston Street, just west of downtown.

Inside the apartment they discovered the body of Peggy Davis, a 29 year old cocktail waitress at the Lucky Lady Club on E. Second Street. Not so lucky for Davis, who had been battered with a hammer and stabbed multiple times.

The Lucky Lady Club was *one of those places.* A short walk from the more mainstream (respectable) hotel/casinos that lined Reno's N. Virginia Street, the Lucky Lady jacked up the price of drinks, and got away with it. The place offered topless dancers on a stage not much larger than the hood of the big boat Cadillacs favored by circa 1970s pimps. Jiggling on stage was only part of it. A clever girl could make a lot of extra money by encouraging customers to buy her a drink. Hers was full price and watered down; with it came a chit. At the end of the night she turned in her chits and counted up her cash.

It's never enough. And some girls always wanted more. So they turned tricks out at Mustang Ranch to supplement the income. Rae Wood was one of these. It didn't take Reno police long to find her.

She was lounging by the pool when they came to arrest her for Davis' murder. Known as the Snake Lady, because she used a snake in her *act* at the Lucky Lady, Wood threw a blouse and slacks over her bikini and was ready to go.

The case was sordid. Davis had once been the girlfriend of Morey Kaplan, owner of the Lucky Lady. When police arrested her, Marjorie Carter talked. And what an interesting story she told.

According to Carter Kaplan had been the mastermind. First he had talked Davis into buying a $100,000 life insurance policy for herself. Just how he did this is anyone's guess. Once she agreed, and made Kaplan her beneficiary, Davis' fate was sealed.

But he didn't want to get his own hands dirty. So he enlisted the services of prostitutes Raye Wood and Marjorie Carter to do the killing.

Carter got herself a plea bargain and was permitted to plead guilty to 2nd degree murder in exchange for testifying against Kaplan at the grand jury and at trial.

Morey Kaplan was found guilty and sentenced to life in prison. Raye Wood was found guilty and sentenced to life in prison. Marjorie Carter got fifteen years. Kaplan appealed to the Nevada Supreme Court and had his sentence overturned. He walked away a free man. Both Carter and Wood have long since been paroled.

The Murder of Oscar Bonavena

In Nevada parlance, the word *ranch* is a euphemism for a whorehouse. When a man says he is going to the ranch a very different thought comes to mind than if he were to say, "I'm going to the whorehouse."

Joe Conforte is credited with starting it all. He didn't of course. Prostitution has been going on in Nevada since before the state became a state. But Conforte did own and operate Nevada's first legal brothel, the Mustang Ranch which became one of the most famous whorehouses in the world. Conforte and his wife Sally saw to that. Neither was the least bit ashamed of how they bankrolled the good life they lived.

To the outsider it was all glamour and allure and beautiful young women who made themselves available…for a price. That was the slick side. The side the Confortes presented to the world. But there was the other side. Drug abuse, alcohol abuse, suicide and murder were not unknown to women who chose the profession.

The lucky ones met and married *a nice guy* and moved on. The not so lucky grew old, a curse worse than death in the business of prostitution. Ten years older than Joe, Sally Conforte eventually grew old. And Joe's attention wandered to other, younger women.

If this bothered her, Sally Conforte kept it to herself. Until she met the handsome heavyweight boxer Oscar Bonavena, who happened to be 26 years younger than she was. And Sally was smitten. In 1975 Joe brought Argentinian Bonavena to Reno to promote fights and to train at the Mustang Ranch property. It had been a very long time since a man flirted with Sally. She liked the attention when Oscar Bonavena noticed her. Before long the two of them were openly flirting with each other.

A contract making, Sally Conforte his manager, was signed. She knew nothing about boxing. But that didn't seem to matter. Sally became Oscar Bonavena's *sugar mama*; he indulged in the good life and gained weight...not good for a boxer.

The lopsided romance might have ended as quickly as it had begun, with no harm-no foul, if Oscar Bonavena hadn't decided he would own the Mustang Ranch. His attention to Sally hadn't fired up Joe. But when he circulated among guests at the Mustang Ranch's grand opening, asking how they liked *his place*, Joe was incensed. Oscar could have Sally, but no one was going to take the Mustang Ranch from him.

Within days of the grand opening, Sally and Oscar were tossed off the property and told not to return. In their absence Oscar's belongings were ransacked and burned. Sally and Oscar traveled to San Francisco to get him a new passport and then headed back to Reno. Early in the morning of May 22, 2976 Oscar Bonavena made a decision that cost him his life.

Intent on confronting Joe, he drove to the Mustang Ranch. At the property's front gate, he demanded to speak to Joe Conforte. One of the guards ordered him to leave. The other guard, Ross Brymer held a high power rifle on him. Oscar Bonavena stepped around his car. As he did so, one of the guards fired his weapon, sending a bullet hurling through Bonavena's heart.

Ross Brymer pled guilty to voluntary manslaughter and served only 15 months in the Nevada State Prison. He died in 2000 at the age of 55.

Hot Tub Murder

Man is the cruelest animal. Friedrich Nietzsche

How much is a life worth? That depends on who you're asking. For Randy Howard and Valerie Fuentes the price of former Sparks city Councilman Val Galleron's life was two thousand dollars and an old motor home. That's what they were paid to do Janine Hillman's dirty work at Galleron's mobile home on the southeast edge of Reno one June night in 1987.

Galleron had a nice little set up on the corner of Model Way and Karen Street. He'd built himself a viewing platform out back of his home; there he sometimes spent hours airplane watching, the runway was yards away, just across Pamela Street. In his garden was a throwback from that time in the 1950s when *Ricky loved Lucy*, a cheery little clay burro planter, with side pouches for plants and greenery. It was home.

And on this warm night in June, he eagerly welcomed the trio into his modest home, glad for the company. He knew Janine Hillman, an attractive woman he'd met and befriended in one of the local bars. There was no reason to mistrust her or the young man and woman she introduced as *friends* Randy and Valerie.

A few drinks and the night wore on. Too late Val Galleron sensed danger. Without warning, Janine Hillman's personality did an about face. Gone was the affable woman he'd enjoyed conversing with. There was no more talk; she wanted his money. And she meant to have it. Fear must have surged through him with the realization that these three meant to do him harm.

Who would hear him if he cried out for help? His mobile home was situated in the Rewana Farms area near the Reno Tahoe Airport runway. The noise of arriving and departing passenger jets was a constant in this small neighborhood; those who lived here long enough learned to close out sounds. Screaming would be worthless.

Janine Hillman's eyes glittered with greed as Howard and Fuentes pawed through Galleron's possessions. He was old and no match for this trio. The stun gun Howard wielded frightened him; Hillman began shouting at him to give her all his money...or else. Howard turned the stun gun on him. Pain shot through Galleron's entire body. Howard and Fuentes tied him up. Hillman demanded money. What he had was in the bank. She would take checks. The old man was untied and handed a pen and his checkbook. Write the checks or else. And hovering over him, they forced him to write checks in the amount of $40,000 to Janine Hillman. In a halting scrawl he signed and dated the checks.

Without warning, Howard and Fuentes grabbed him by the arms and shoved him into his hot tub. On so many other nights the hot tub had been his relief for tired and aching muscles. Not tonight.

Throughout the evening his television had provided a steady stream of changing scenes, words and music. No one noticed. From the hot tub he might have glanced at the TV and wished for normalcy. He might even have allowed himself a glimmer of hope; surely they would soon go away. But Valentine Galleron hadn't counted on the heartless cruelty of these three. As he cowered in the hot tub, Howard and Fuentes picked up his television and tossed it into the water with him.

With their victim dead in his hot tub, the three killers divvied up their take; Janine Hillman had checks totaling $40,000 dollars and Howard and Fuentes got the keys to his motor home plus $2000.00. The next morning Janine Hillman set out for the bank and Randy Howard and Valerie Fuentes set out for San Diego in the dead man's motor home. Hillman persuaded the bank that she was Galleron's daughter, stuffed the forty grand in her purse and went on with her life. So did Howard and Fuentes in San Diego.

When Galleron's body was discovered family noted that his motor home was missing. Police began the search that would lead to the arrest of Howard and Fuentes. Within days Hillman was also behind bars. She might have been tight lipped. But Howard and Fuentes were talking.

On July 26, 1987 Randy Howard and Valerie Fuentes plead guilty to the murder of Valentine Galleron. Janine Hillman would tough it out and stand trial. Like Randy Howard and Valerie Fuentes, she was found guilty of first degree murder and sentenced to life without the possibility of parole.

Fast forward to 1994, Valerie Fuentes dies at the Nevada State Women's Prison. Three years later, 42 year old Randy Howard was asking for a parole and singing a different song, *the killing was all Valerie. She did it.*

Fast forward 2017…Inmate number 25689, Janine Hillman ended up a sad faced old woman who continued to seek parole. And Val Galleron's family continued to thwart her efforts. They no longer have to worry about that.

Hillman, who was serving two life sentences at the Florence McClure Women's Correctional Center in Las Vegas, died at the Valley Hospital Medical Center on October 30, 2017.

Baby

Kathaleena Draper was seventeen, pregnant and unwed. There was no way she could take care of a baby; she could barely take care of herself. Her maternal aunt Erin Rae Kuhn-Brown wanted a baby desperately. So they worked out the perfect solution all around, Kathaleena would leave Las Vegas and move in with her aunt in Sacramento. There she would await the birth of the child her aunt was eager to adopt.

It was March; the baby was due in five months. While Kathaleena made plans for her return to Vegas after the birth, Erin happily bought *baby things* and prepared the nursery for the impending arrival of *her* baby. She'd attempted adoption a few times before, only to meet with failure. This time things would be different for the thirty-one year old divorcee. Lost in her own happiness, Erin Kuhn-Brown didn't stop to think that the teenage Kathaleena might change her mind. But the further along she got, the more Kathaleena questioned the decision to give up her child.

Kuhn-Brown's dreams of motherhood came crashing down around her with Kathaleena's announcement that she had changed her mind, and intended on keeping her baby. Kuhn-Brown wasn't about to let her niece keep *her* baby from her. Their arguments were constant, heated and loud. Finally Kuhn gave in. She would drive Kathaleena, now eight months pregnant, home to Las Vegas and forget about the adoption.

On June 16, 2000 they loaded Kuhn-Brown's blue Taurus and headed out on I-80 east toward Reno. When they arrived in Fernley thirty miles past Reno, Kuhn-Brown stopped at the Lazy Inn Motel on Main Street promising Kathaleena that they would get a good night's rest before driving on. But Kuhn-Brown had other plans. After settling into room number 123, she announced that she needed a few things at the store.

Kathaleena was sound asleep when her aunt pressed a pillow over her face. Thinking she was dead, Kuhn-Brown began slicing into Kathaleena's stomach. She would take the baby. At that point Kathaleena may have awakened. The autopsy showed that the teenager died of asphyxiation because a surgical glove had been shoved down into her throat.

Kathaleena was dead. The baby was not. And the baby was all that mattered to Kuhn-Brown. She cut the baby from its mother's womb and held it aloft; a boy. Her joy was short lived; the baby would not survive another hour. After cleaning up the blood and gore in the motel room, Kuhn-Brown put the baby in a garbage bag. His body was left alongside a lonely road just outside of Fernley. Her niece's body was wrapped in a shower curtain and dumped on the side of a highway just outside of Sacramento, California.

An anonymous tip led police to Erin Rae Kuhn-Brown's doorstep. She led police to the spot where she'd left the baby's body, but refused to waive extradition to Nevada. Several days later Governor Gray Davis approved Nevada's request to extradite Kuhn-Brown to Nevada where she would stand trial for the murder of her niece and unborn child.

At her hearing, Kuhn-Brown pleaded guilty to two counts of murder thus avoiding the death penalty. She is currently serving her sentence at the Florence McClure Women's Correctional Center in Las Vegas.

Too Young to Die

Dear Mother
You once said that I didn't deserve you and if I did anything wrong you would leave me. You don't have to now, for I am. Don't worry about me because I have a job and can buy my own things now. You probably won't see me again, at least until I am 18. Here is that hat for Jerry. He can have my toys and my funny books that are in the back of your car.

These were the last words Barbara Hopman wrote to her mother. Within the week Barbara would be dead. Shot and killed by her sixteen-year-old boyfriend in a downtown Reno hotel room, she would never have the opportunity to do any of the things that girls of the early 1950's dreamed of doing. She may have looked older than her years, but Barbara Hopman was only thirteen years old.

Barbara's family was living in Tracy California only a short time before she met Pat Chavez Alvillar at a school football game. The attraction was immediate. Within the week they were inseparable and going steady. Had they known, Barbara's parents would certainly have disapproved. But they were not aware of the budding romance. And so it continued.

Two days before Thanksgiving Pat suggested that they run away and get married in Reno. Barbara readily agreed. The pretty redhead was just as tired of parental rules as her boyfriend was. As they made their plans Pat insisted that his best friend, Carl Cecil Wofford be included in their adventure. Barbara liked

Carl. As long as she and Pat were going to be together, she didn't mind if he tagged along.

Barbara packed her suitcases, left the note for her mother, and crept out of the house. She never intended on coming back.

The trio boarded the bus for Reno with forty dollars tucked safely in Barbara's purse. Neither Pat nor Carl had any cash. They would shoplift and steal anything else they needed. Reno was the epitome of glamour, and excitement; they had heard adults brag about their adventures in Reno often enough and now the teenagers were ready to have some fun of their own.

Sunrise was a few hours away when the bus rolled into the depot on Center Street. The three teenagers had made their escape from parents and their rules; they were finally in Reno. The boys had only a few items, but Barbara had brought two suitcases filled with her favorite sweaters and skirts.

Leaving her luggage with the two boys, she walked to the nearby Overland Hotel. Later the desk clerk would say that the teenager had asked about room rates, and when told what they were, said she would have to check with her husband first. Moments later she returned with Pat in tow.

They registered as Mr. and Mrs. and were given a room key. Within the hour Carl appeared at the hotel desk and registered for his own room. The clerk asked him if he knew the other young couple and he said, "They're my cousins. We're on our way to Elko to look for work."

Forty dollars could not last forever, even in 1952. After a night at the Overland, the teenagers looked at their cash and decided to rent one room at a cheaper hotel. This time they chose the Menlo Hotel on Commercial Row. Across from the train depot, the hotel was indeed cheaper.

For the next five days they would live their lives in Room three of the Menlo Hotel, or on the streets of downtown Reno. During the day they snatched purses, shoplifted, and ate hamburgers and milkshakes at the drugstores. When the streets got too cold they scurried back to their room where they read comic books and snacked candy bars and sodas.

Bored with the confines of the small hotel room the three teenagers set out to explore Reno again; snow crunched under their feet as they walked under the Reno arch and down N. Virginia Street toward the Riverside Hotel.

The boys made snowballs and tossed them at each other. Barbara half-heartedly joined in. She was more interested in window shopping and stopped to gaze in at what each shop had to offer. Christmas was three weeks away; merchants displayed their finest items in exquisitely decorated settings. Dressed in fine woolen winter wear, blank faced mannequins stood amid paper snow and foil icicles.

December 2, 1952, they walked on until they came to a jewelry store. Barbara stared longingly at the flashing diamond rings on display. Pat tugged on her coat sleeve. They'd stood at the window long enough; he was tired of looking at rings. He wanted to look in the sporting goods store. Carl chided him about buying her a ring, and he agreed that he would one-day...

Barbara was hungry and tired. They stopped and got sandwiches and she went back to the hotel room alone. Hours later the boys returned with a gun Pat had stolen.

"Look what I got." He bragged waving the gun at her.

Barbara stared at the gun in silence. She'd been waiting in the room for a long time.

"You been two timing me?" He demanded playfully pointing the gun at her. She shook her head no. He acted different when Carl was around. Pat slapped her across the mouth, then pulled her to him and kissed her.

"Better not ever two time me!" He laughed.

"We stole some Vodka." Carl explained.

"Yeah we did." Pat laughed.

Carl stretched out on his own bed and was quickly engrossed in his comic book.

But Pat was not done with his game of Russian roulette. "Do you love me?" He asked Carl, pointing the gun at him.

"'Yeah whatever you say." Carl chuckled absently.

Pat pulled the trigger. There was only one bullet in the gun. Carl had escaped. Someone knocked on the door.

"The manager says to quiet down in there or else, said a voice from the other side of the door.

"Okay." Carl replied. "We will."

Pat turned to Barbara. Pointing the gun at her, he demanded, "Do you love me?"

"Yes…but sometimes I don't."

Smiling, he pulled the trigger. The single bullet crashed into Barbara's forehead, killing her instantly. Her body fell to the floor between the two beds.

"My God! What have you done?" Carl screamed.

Pat opened the window and threw the gun onto the roof.

"Pat! You can't throw the gun away."

"Let's say it was suicide. Yeah! She killed herself."

"We can't tell a lie like that!"

"We got to Carl! We can say that she was worried I was going to leave her."

"Alright, but we better call the police."

Carl ran out of the room and cornered the man who'd just knocked at their door. "Someone's been shot! Get the police!"

The girl's body lay crumpled in the space between the two beds. Blood poured from the wound in her head. Carl crawled out onto the roof and retrieved the gun.

"This what shot her?" One of the officers asked.

Carl nodded silently, his gaze on Barbara. "I think I'm going to be sick. All this blood is making me sick."

The story the two boys told sounded farfetched to investigators. The girl had calmly put the gun to her head and committed suicide when she decided one of them didn't love her anymore. It didn't add up.

The drive from the Menlo Hotel to the police station was a short one. In that time the boys' story changed. Barbara's death had been a horrible accident, a deadly game of Russian roulette. A paraffin test bore the story out. There was no residue on either Barbara's or Carl's hands. Pat was arrested for murder and Carl as a material witness.

Barbara's death would mark the first time in its history, that the Reno Police Department used color film to photograph a crime scene.

Somewhere out in the darkness between Reno and Tracy, Mr. and Mrs. Hopman made their way toward the city to pick up their runaway daughter. They knew where she was because a friend had seen her in Reno days before. In the predawn hours, they arrived at the Reno Police Department smiling and joking and looking for their errant only daughter...

In Tracy a ringing phone would wake the Alvillars from sound sleep. It would be the last such sleep they would know for a very long time.

Carl was sentenced to the boys' reformatory at Elko; nearly a year after Barbara's death Pat was permitted to plead guilty to voluntary manslaughter. His sentence was one to five years at the Nevada State Prison in Carson City. At sixteen, he was the youngest inmate the prison had housed since Floyd Burton Loveless who was executed at seventeen on September 29, 1944.
Because of his youth the warden assigned Pat to the state farm where he worked with other trustees taking care of the prison's livestock. According to the warden, "Pat did a man's job" and was a hard worker.

I Hear Voices...

Aside from for her mother and her three year old son, Erline Folker had no family in Las Vegas. The pretty divorcee's father and his large family were all back in Washington, where she'd been born and raised. Erline (Childers) graduated in the Walla Walla high school class of 1953, fell in love and got married. Typical of the early 1950s, lee so in the era of *Father Knows Best* and *Leave it to Beaver*, was the divorce that left Erline alone with a young son to raise.

Erline came to Las Vegas, hoping for a fresh start, and moved in her mother. She took a job as a stenographer at a stationery store. It paid the bills and kept them fed. The divorce hadn't been easy, but she was starting to date again. Life was good. Then on afternoon of November 3, 1958 Erline Folker encountered madness.

Jack Rainsberger had been in and out of trouble since he was 12 years old. At 23 that encompassed half his life. The Los Angeles handyman had no friends. Whenever he did converse with his co-workers and employers, the subject was so esoteric, that he became known as a *genius.*

Rainsberger came to Las Vegas because the *voices* ordered him to do so. These voices also demanded that he select a victim for his human sacrifice. He was looking for just such a victim when he glanced into the window of the stationery store and saw Erline Folker. She would be his sacrifice. He roamed around the neighborhood and waited for her to get off work.

Late in the afternoon, she covered her typewriter and tidied her desk. Telling her co-workers that she'd see them *tomorrow*, Erline walked out the door. Rainsberger followed her to her car. He was quick. Before she realized what was happening, he pressed a knife against her back and shoved her into the car. Still holding the knife against her, he crawled into the backseat, and ordered her to drive out to the desert. Erline Folker would never be seen alive again.

That night Jack Rainsberger went to the Las Vegas Police Station and filed a robbery report. He claimed that he'd been robbed and left to walk miles in the desert. The next morning Erline's mother filed a missing person's report; her daughter had not come home all night. This wasn't like her. Before the police could investigate the robbery, or the missing woman's whereabouts, a bus driver discovered a body in the desert. Erline Folker's body was clad in the tweed skirt and blouse she'd worn to work the day before. Her underclothes were wrapped around her neck. The woman's throat had been slit from ear to ear.

With news of the discovery of Erline Folker's body Jack Rainsberger had a story to share. He confessed to the murder. He told officers that the voices had told him to find a human sacrifice.

"I saw her in the stationery store and decided she would be my victim. I followed her to her car and made her drive to the desert. Then I sacrificed her. It was all part of a regular ritual, but I can't tell you how I go through it."

Rainsberger was convicted of Folker's murder and sentenced to die. He would spend the next 13 years of his life on Nevada's death row---waiting for (and appealing) that appointment with the gas chamber. Then in 1972 the death penalty was brought before the Supreme Court in *Furman v. Georgia, Jackson v. Georgia*, and *Branch v. Texas* (known collectively as the landmark case *Furman v. Georgia* (408 U.S. 238)) On June 29, 1972, the Court voided 40 death penalty statutes, commuting the sentences of 629 death row inmates across the US and suspending the death penalty.

Jack Rainsberger, who wrote poetry and created crossword puzzles, now had reason to hope that someday he might be a free man. Over the next several years, he would suffer a heart attack, attend 19 unsuccessful parole hearings in which Erline Folker's son would also appear. Eventually Rainsberger would be set free to live out his life in Reno. He died there at the age of 72.

The Murder of Brianna Denison

February 15, 2008 the day after Valentine's Day. Just another day in Reno, bargain hunters made their way through stores in search of half off chocolates and other items associated with the day of romance. The promise of spring hung in the air as mild daytime temperatures rose to the average 50 degree mark. This was the day that the search for Brianna Denison would come to an end.

Brianna had been missing since January 21st. She hadn't let willingly. What young woman would leave her home without her purse, her shoes, or more importantly her cell phone? Her friends and family had held out hope that the pretty 19 year old would be found and brought home to them. But those who worked in law enforcement knew the odds. The chances of finding her alive diminished with each passing day.

Eight days after Brianna's disappearance a woman came forward with a story about someone who'd been raped at gunpoint at the University of Nevada Reno a year earlier. Male DNA found on the couch Brianna had slept on the night she was abducted would match the DNA in two recent sexual attacks in the university area.

Because Brianna was believed to be a kidnap victim, the FBI joined the search that involved more than a thousand volunteers who combed through the city and surrounding desert areas in their quest to bring Brianna home. Among those helping in the search was Dawn Gibbons, Nevada's first lady.

Because blue was Brianna's favorite color blue ribbons were hung throughout the Reno area as a symbol. Photographs of Brianna were posted throughout the area. As volunteers worked round the clock, vigils were held in the hopes she would come home safely. Brianna was a hometown girl. She became Reno's daughter, granddaughter, sister, and loved one.

In the end it wasn't one of those who searched for her, but a man returning from his lunch break who discovered her body in a field near his job in south Reno. Lying near her body was a pair of woman's black thong under panties. They would provide both female and male DNA

Investigators descended on the field. Right behind them were the local news teams. The Denison family's worst fears had been confirmed. The lifeless body was that of their beloved Brianna. While the family endured the pain of sudden senseless loss, investigators went to work catching the killer.

Grief stricken, the Denison family remained proactive. They formed the Bring Bri Justice Foundation dedicated to the apprehension of Brianna's killer, and to the safety of all women and children.

The girlfriend of twenty-seven year old James Biela confided in a friend that she had found another woman's panties in Biela's truck. Not sure just what this meant, she had demanded an explanation from Biela. At his trial she would testify that she he hadn't given her a "straight answer."

The friend was suspicious. She wondered if Biela might be responsible for Brianna's death. So she reported the information to Reno's Secret Witness tip line. This was the break investigators needed.

Police interviewed Biela, and asked if he would submit to a DNA test. He refused. But his girlfriend permitted their son's DNA to be taken and compared. The child's DNA had a familial match to that found in the panties left with Brianna Denison's body.

On November 25, 2008 Biela was dropping his son off at a Reno area daycare when police arrested him. He was charged with murder, sexual assault and first degree kidnapping. A sample of his DNA was taken. Reno Police had their man. A sigh of relief echoed across the community.

Unfortunately James Biela is not the only monster in our midst. In its mission state the Bring Bri Foundation stated that it is committed to the safety of all women and children in Nevada in the memory of Brianna Denison.

James Biela was found guilty on all counts. And after deliberating nine hours the jury handed down the death sentence. At this writing Biela is on death row awaiting an execution date at Ely State Prison in White Pine County Nevada.

The Denison family continued their fight. In 2013 they won a hard fought battle to see Brianna's Law enacted in the Nevada Legislature. As he signed SB 243, Governor Brian Sandoval called it an historic day. And it was. Brianna's Law mandates that all probable cause felony arrests include a cheek swab and cross referenced with DNA from other crime scenes.

After Biela was sentenced to death, Brianna's mother Bridgette Denison said. "When James Michael Biela messed with my little girl, he messed with the wrong families... the wrong women, and the wrong city and state."

Indeed he had.

Dancer

Sorry Hollywood, Las Vegas is *the Entertainment Capital of the World.* Back in the day, those seeking glamour and fame struck out for Hollywood in hopes of making it big in the movies. Times change; todays more hip generation sees Las Vegas as *the* place to see and be seen, *the* place to make it big. So it was with Debbie Flores-Narvaez, a beautiful and talented young woman who left

Maryland for Sin City with high hopes and big dreams. By early 2010 those dreams were coming true and she was living the Vegas lifestyle.

Debbie had danced her way from a go-go dancer at the Rain nightclub in the Palms to a stage role in the popular Fantasy Revue at the Luxor. She was in a relationship with dancer Jason Omar Griffith. Griffith, who went by the professional name Blu, had an equally great gig in Cirque de Soleil's Beatles' LOVE at the Mirage.

It might have been perfect---if only Blu had been as committed to her as she was to him. He wasn't. There were other women, and this was something Debbie, whose loyalty was boundless, could not accept. And yet the tempestuous on-again-off-again relationship continued. An abortion and later a violent argument in October 2010 changed everything between them. The fight ended with Debbie being kicked and thrown to the floor. Blu was arrested and charged with domestic violence. Now the Puerto Rican beauty was finally through with him. Or was she? They continued seeing each other sporadically even though he couldn't be monogamous.

Thirteen days before Christmas 2010, Debbie drove to Blu's place to watch the season finale of *Dexter* with him. It was the last time she would ever be seen alive.

It was not like her to be a *no/call no/show*. A dedicated dancer, she realized the importance of rehearsals. But she had blown the midnight rehearsal off without so much as a text. Likewise the 5PM Monday performance. Where was she? When an out of state friend learned of Debbie's no show, she knew that something had to be wrong. The woman called the Las Vegas Metropolitan Police Department and asked for their help in locating her friend. The last she'd heard, Debbie was going to her ex-boyfriend's place to watch *Dexter*.

MISSING
Debbie Flores Narvaez
www.bringdebbiehome.com

DESCRIPTION
Hispanic
Brown Hair
Brown Eyes
Age: 31
Height: 5'5"
Weight: 125lbs
Missing From: Las Vegas, NV
Last known sighting was on
Dec. 12 around 7 p.m.,
when she left her Vegas
home to visit an ex-boyfriend
driving her maroon, four-door
1997 Chevrolet Prism.

**Anyone with information of her whereabouts is encouraged to contact
Metro's Missing Person Unit at 707-828-2907
or Crime Stoppers at 702-385-5555
Help Us Bring Her Home**

When questioned, the boyfriend knew nothing. Last he'd seen her she was fine and driving away in her Prism. No, they hadn't watched *Dexter* together. But when her roommate called police to report Debbie and her car missing, she also told them about the plan to watch the television show. The Prism was found later that day, but there was no sign of Debbie Flores-Narvaez. Where was she? That was the question on everyone's mind. Days went by; friends and family continued to hope for her safe return. A joyless Christmas came and went. The days turned into weeks. Fliers and missing person posters of the vivacious Debbie were put out seeking the public's help in locating her. Surely someone knew something. Someone did.

Debbie Flores-Narvaez had been missing for 24 days when a witness came forward on January 5, 2011. The former girlfriend of Jason Omar Griffith gave a damning statement concerning the disappearance of the dancer. On December 15th 2010 Blu had asked her if he could store some things at her place. She told him that her apartment was small, but if his stuff would fit in the closet or the patio, he was welcome to do so.

The next thing she knew, Griffith and a friend were unloading a large plastic tub from a U-Haul truck. Upon closer inspection, she noticed that the tub was filled with a dark colored concrete.

She asked him what was in the tub. He ignored her. She asked again. Silence; if he wouldn't tell her what was in the tub, she wasn't about to let him store it at her place.

"Debbie's in there." He said.

One look and she realized he wasn't joking. No! She wasn't going to let him keep *that* here. He and his friend lifted the tub back into the rental truck and left. Had he lied to her? What should she do? Would she meet the same fate if she told what she knew? That thought frightened her. It would be weeks before she finally came forward to tell her story and to share the name of Griffith's friend. Three days later he was at the police department and asking for a deal. After assurances of leniency for his part in helping Griffith dispose of the remains, he began to talk…and he knew every gruesome detail. What's more he was willing to tell police where they could find the body, still encased in a plastic tub.

Debbie-Flores Narvaez, he said, came to Blu's place to watch *Dexter* on the night of December 12th. Like always, Debbie and Blu started to fight. He left them to it at around 8:30. When he returned to the house hours later, Blu informed him that he had killed Debbie accidently. Now he needed to dispose of the body. They stuffed the body into a tub, filled it with concrete and put it in the garage to harden overnight.

Next day they rented a truck and moved the tub to the house of a friend who was out of the country. There, they found that the tub was leaking so they broke it open with a sledgehammer. Blu then took a hacksaw and sawed off both of Flores-Narvaez' legs. Finished, he placed the legs in a separate tub from body, and filled each with fresh concrete.

Griffith was convicted of second degree murder in the death of Debbie Flores-Narvaez. In July 2014, Judge Kathleen Delaney handed down the maximum sentence, 10 years to life imprisonment. His lawyers plan to appeal to the Nevada Supreme Court.

Micaela

In his 1993 boo*k 100 Best Small Towns in America*, Norman Crampton named Elko, in the northeastern part of Nevada, as one such town. It's been great PR for the city that combined with nearby Spring Creek, has a population of fewer than 50,000. Elko is *hometown* Nevada. Elko is rich in mining, western and railroad history it is also home of two popular annual events: The National Cowboy Poetry Gathering and the Basque Festival which honors the Basque heritage of early settlers to this community.

There have been many historic cases played out in the Elko County Courthouse since the city was founded in December 1868. In 1889 Elizabeth Potts and her husband Josiah stood trial for murder here. Convicted, and sentenced to death, the pair was hanged in Elko, very near the site of the present day courthouse. This made Elizabeth Potts the only woman Nevada has ever legally executed. Fifty years later fifteen year old Floyd Loveless was tried in Elko and sentenced to die in the gas chamber for killing Carlin Constable A.H. Berning.

Probably no killer who's ever stood before a judge in these courtrooms is any callous and cruel than two that appeared here in 2012: Kody Cree Patten and Toni Fratto.

West Wendover is a small town that sits on the edge of the Great Salt Lake Desert. It's about an hour outside of Elko, traveling east on I-80. With barely more than 4000 residents, West Wendover is one of those safe little towns where everybody knows everybody, or at least a relative or two. Within this small community are five resort/casinos. Gaming is king here and the town's largest employer.

It was here that Micaela Costanzo lived with her family who made their living in the casinos. Known as Mickey to friends and family, the pretty high school track star was popular and well liked. Among her friends she counted classmates Toni Fratto and Kody Patten who she'd known since childhood. She knew them and trusted them.

Kody had once been her boyfriend. Now he and Toni were an item and living together at her parents' house. He had even converted to Mormonism so that he and Toni could be married one day. But Micaela was texting Kody. Apparently she wanted him back.

This caused the jealous rages that seethed in Toni's heart. Micaela was pretty and athletic and popular. And Kody, Toni thought, might resume their romance. Was he sneaking around to see Micaela? Did he call her? How could she live if Kody should dump her for Micaela?

According to Fratto, Kody Patten picked her and Micaela up at the high school on March 3, 2011 and the three of them drove to the desert outside of West Wendover to talk. Did Micaela sense danger? Fratto would later say that the further they got from town the more agitated Micaela became. At an area known as the gravel pit, Patten parked the car and jumped out, followed by Micaela. Their conversation turned loud. When Fratto heard a thud, she emerged from the vehicle to see Micaela on the ground. "I shoved her away from me and she hit her head." Patten explained.

"Everything from there on out was kind of a blur to me. It went downhill from there." Fratto said in her confession.

Fratto grabbed the shovel they had brought along and slammed it into Micaela's back. Together they slashed, kicked and pummeled the helpless girl. And as she lay dazed and dying, they slit her throat.

They then dug a shallow grave and pushed Micaela into it. Her belongings, they would burn elsewhere.

Fratto and Patten then drove back to West Wendover and went on with their lives. Micaela would be missing for two days before her body was discovered. When police found her phone with text messages to and from Kody Patten they focused attention on him.

As a person of interest he was asked to come to the police department for an interview. During the interview he admitted killing Micaela but made no mention of Fratto.

A month later, Fratto went to Patten's s attorney's office and confessed to having helped Patten murder Micaela Costanzo. She too was charged with first degree murder. But if she would testify against Kody Patten, she would receive a lesser charge. The death penalty would also be off the table.

Toni Cecile Fratto was sentenced to life with the possibility of parole after eighteen years on April 16, 2012. Kody Cree Patten was sentenced to life without the possibility of parole on August 24, 2012. In sentencing Patten, Elko District Court Judge Daniel Papez said, "Your blood runs cold, Mr. Patten. There shall be no possibility of parole."

The one question that neither killer could answer was why? Why had they so savagely and cruelly murdered Micaela Costanzo?

Who Killed Melvin Gordon?

The killer left fingerprints at the scene. And his DNA has been entered into the national database. When, and if, he is ever arrested, there will be no escape from those prints and a DNA match up. Until that time, the murder of Reno's Melvin Gordon goes unsolved and a killer walks free.

September 25, 2002 thousands of motorcyclists were in town for the annual Street Vibrations. Normally quiet streets were filled with the roar of motorcycles.

Radio personality, turned real estate salesman, Melvin Gordon was entertaining at his cluttered Smithridge Park condo in Southeast Reno. According to neighbors there was nothing unusual about this. Those who knew him best knew that Gordon regularly visited Virginia Lake where he picked up agreeable young men. From there he would take them to his condo two miles away for an evening of romance.

Tonight Gordon was very comfortable with his visitor. He removed his socks and shoes and then his shirt. Then something went terribly wrong, Gordon, or his visitor, had misjudged the other's intentions.

A fight ensued. It would end with Melvin Gordon's death in the living room of his forty year old condo. Not content to use just a knife, the killer had also stabbed Gordon with a fork and a letter opener…over and over again. While the fatally wounded Gordon desperately crawled toward the front door and help, the killer rummaged through his home looking for anything of value. Melvin Gordon died there on the living room floor as his killer jumped in his maroon SUV and fled the scene.

A call to 911 led police to the stolen SUV. The killer was probably the driver that witnesses reported as driving recklessly and having sideswiped a parked car on Harvard Way, a street not so very far from Melvin Gordon's condo. But no one knew that at the time.

A police officer tried to pull the SUV over, but he sped off. The desk sergeant instructed the officer to let him go. The officer did so and went on with his shift.

Later that night, the family that had made the original 911 call recognized the maroon SUV parked in the drive through at a local fast food restaurant in Sparks. They stopped and looked inside the abandoned vehicle. A bloody knife and blood, they called the police again. And once again a decision was made that helped a murderer escape. The desk sergeant told the responding officers to park the car and be on their way.

After some argument with their supervisor, the officers did as they were told, noting that the vehicle was registered to Melvin Gordon of Smithridge Park Condos in Reno.

When they arrived at Gordon's condo they discovered his body. The killer's fingerprints and DNA are in databases. The witnesses who made the original 911 call were able to give a description of the man they saw driving Gordon's SUV on the night of the slaying. Perhaps one day this murderer will be apprehended and brought to justice.

The Murder that Changed Reno

There have been many changes to Reno since the city was founded in 1868. None have had any more impact than the brutal 1963 slaying of Sonja McCaskie. The senseless murder put an end to Reno's small town safe no-need-to-lock-the-doors mentality, forever.

A working middleclass neighborhood on Yori Avenue in Southeast Reno was the scene of the horrendous crime. And it's still there, the little duplex that Sonja McCaskie bought for herself and her infant son. Those who live there probably have no idea what that took place in the tiny rear bedroom one spring night.

April 4, 1963. She was tired. And after a quick shower she went to bed early. She forgot to lock her back door…the carelessness would cost her life

It was nearing midnight when he pulled up to the curb. Every house on the block was dark; the street was silent. Its residents were early to bed and early to rise. No one would see him. He crept around to the backyard. Her dainty lace underwear was hanging on the clothesline. He stepped on the concrete slab back porch and pulled off his socks and shoes. Then, carefully wrapping a pair of black panties around his hand, he turned the door handle of Sonja McCaskie's duplex. It was unlocked.

He found her there in her bedroom, sleeping soundly.

He unwound a length of twine and wrapped it around her neck, then straddled the sleeping woman. He pulled the twine tighter as he raped her. Angered at the rasping noise rising up from his victim's throat, he pulled the butcher knife from his waistband and thrust it into her throat; again and again and again. And then, according to the killer, "You might say I went berserk."

He spent the next several hours in the duplex dismembering and decapitating Sonja McCaskie while he listened to her records. In the living room, he looked down at his victim's headless body; he was not finished yet. After hacking off her left foot and cutting out her heart, he was spent.

He shoved the body into the hope chest, and tossed the head in afterwards. "Like you would a basketball" He would later confess. He turned the mattress over and made the bed with fresh sheets.

When Sonja McCaskie didn't show up for work in the office at the meat packing plant in Sparks, the supervisor knew it was odd behavior for the normally punctual young woman. Car trouble, perhaps, he thought.

As the hours ticked by with still no sign of Sonja, the babysitter grew uneasy. When she called Sonja's job and was told that no one had seen her since yesterday, uneasiness gave way to fear. She called the house several more times only to hear the continual ringing. It wasn't like the young mother, who was always so good about being on time. Another hour came and went. Finally, she picked up the phone and called the police

As the police cruiser rolled up to the duplex on Yori Avenue early in that evening, the officers noticed nothing out of the ordinary in the quiet neighborhood. The black and white glare of television sets could be seen through several windows, a baby cried somewhere and dogs barked in the distance. The house they were sent to was dark…and silent.

Their flashlights circled the yard, nothing seemed amiss. They front door was slightly ajar. They knocked once; "Reno Police Department" They called and walked in on horror.

With only the light of their flashlights to guide them they could see the blood spatters on the wall, the sofa, the floor; this was not a routine call. One of the officers stooped to pick up a cloth bundle, out rolled a foot. Nearby lay a human heart. The officer stepped out on the front porch to gag. Neither had ever encountered anything like this; doubtful anyone at the Reno PD had.

In the cedar chest officers discovered a headless body with knives protruding from it; the body looked more like a mannequin than that of a human being. Beneath the body lay the head, wrapped in a white lace tablecloth. They called for crime scene personnel and cordoned off the duplex.

"This is the very worst case we have ever had." Reno Police Chief Elmer Briscoe.

Modern forensics with its use of DNA analysis was decades away. Except for a bloody footprint there was nothing to identify the killer. But with the print, they would know him, when they had him. A week passed; police got their break when one of the downtown pawnshops reported that someone had hocked a camera like the one they were looking for. The young man had signed his name and his address on the pawn tag.

Several police cars converged on the run down house on Neil Road, less than seven blocks from the home of Sonja McCaskie. Elza Bean opened the door to the officers and denied any knowledge of the murder; his eighteen year old son Tom admitted he had hocked the camera and agreed to accompany them to the police department.

In his rambling 63 page confession the only explanation Bean could offer were the words, "To rape a girl has been a dream of mine since childhood."

An eighteen year old boy was responsible for the heinous crime that had focused worldwide attention on Reno. Newsmen from across the globe came to catch a glimpse of the youthful killer; many of them would return in July to cover his trial. Renoites were shocked. Students and teachers at Earl Wooster High School where he was a student were stunned at the news of Tom Bean's arrest. He was quiet and kept to himself, still the school wasn't that large and many of them knew him.

On July 8, 1963 Thomas Lee Bean was convicted of first degree murder in the death of Sonja McCaskie. He was sentenced to die in the gas chamber sometime the following September. After his sentencing Bean was taken to the Nevada State prison in Carson City. He appealed his sentence and by 1972 had spent more time on death row than any other inmate. That same year, in Furman v. Georgia the Supreme Court struck down the death penalty. The de facto moratorium on the death penalty led to Bean being released of the death penalty and given life without parole.

At this writing he has been an inmate at the Nevada State Prison longer than any other inmate.

David Blackwell photo Courtesy of the Nevada State Library and Archives

Cop Killer

Only eighteen years old, David Blackwell was destined for a date with the gas chamber. He broke out of the Washington State Reformatory on October 13, 1947 and headed to Reno. Three weeks later he and an accomplice were in town and looking for an easy place to rob. They decided on Charlie's Bar on South Virginia St.

They waited until the bar was nearly deserted, then walked in and sat at opposite ends of the bar. Bartender/owner, Charles Frisch took their orders and turned back to the tap where he expertly drew two beers, topping each with a thick layer of foam. A hint of a smile crossed his face as he placed the beer before the two young men. Neither of them returned his smile; instead they pulled their guns and stared coldly at him.

Before Frisch could react, Blackwell, who was nearest the door jumped up and locked the front door. "You're closed mister." He snapped. While the customers watched aghast, he grabbed the telephone and yanked it from the wall.

"Just be quiet and no one will get hurt." He assured them.

His accomplice leapt across the bar and opened the cash register. "Where's the rest of it?" He demanded of Frisch, who pointed toward a small cabinet. Carrying a sack full of silver and all the money from the register, they ran to the back door. And with the warning, "Everyone stay here and no one try to follow us," the two robbers fled.

While the police investigated the Charlie's Bar holdup, the Highway 40 Tavern was being robbed in much the same manner. The take for both robberies was hefty and estimated to be around $3000.00.

Police had descriptions of the two men and knew they were both young and tall. That wasn't much to go on. On Friday night Sgts. Gene Cowan and Daryl Read canvassed local hotels for anyone matching the robbers' descriptions. At the Carlton Hotel on Sierra Street, they discovered that three young men had recently registered in a suite.

Cowan and Read notified Reno Night Police Captain Roy Geach and Sgt. Allen Glass and the four officers met shortly before midnight in the lobby of the Carlton Hotel. Geach and Glass knew the Biggest Little City's mean streets, between them they had racked up seventeen years on the Reno Police force. Within the past year both men had been promoted to a higher rank. Geach, the older of the two by twenty years, was a former train engineer and legislature from Esmeralda County.

Glass came to the department after tiring of his job in a local department store. It was a decision he'd never regretted. While he was working for the police department, World War II broke out. He left the force to enlist in the Navy. After being honorably discharged Glass returned to Reno and his job as a patrolman.

With more people in town and on the streets, Friday nights were always long and tiring. Their shift was winding down. Hopefully they could make an arrest before calling it a day. Putting the men responsible for the recent armed robberies, behind bars was uppermost in their minds as the four men quickly walked upstairs to the second floor. The last thing Reno needed was more criminals.

Read knocked loudly on the room door. "Reno Police department open up!"

Silence; he knocked again…and again. Finally the door slowly opened and a young man peered out at them.

"Yeah whadya want?" He asked with a smirk. In answer Cowan and Read pushed their way into the room and shoved him against the door. He reached for his pocket. They were wise to that maneuver. They pounced on him, relieving him of his gun in the process.

Glass and Geach quickly surveyed the room, nice suite, and expensive. The adjoining room's door was wide open. From where they stood, the two officers could see someone wrapped in covers, lying on the bed.

They stepped into the room. Geach grabbed the covers and pulled them back. Suddenly the sound of gunfire exploded in the room as David Blackwell rose up shooting wildly. Both Roy Geach and Allen Glass were struck several times. Glass fell to the floor mortally wounded. Geach would die in an ambulance enroute to the Washoe Medical Center.

Cowan returned Blackwell's fire; when a bullet hit him in the shoulder, Blackwell dropped his gun and cried, "You've hit me. I'm through."

One of the accomplices was placed under arrest and taken to the county jail, the other was arrested when he arrived at the hotel room later. David Blackwell was taken to the Washoe Medical Center suffering from a non-critical gunshot wound. While he recovered in the hospital, his father arrived from Tacoma Washington.

"I intend to get to the bottom of this—find out all the circumstances and give my boy all the help I can." The elder Blackwell informed police.

No one could blame a parent for coming to the aid of his child. But Reno Police Chief Clayton Phillips kindly told him that young Blackwell had already admitted killing the two policemen and had signed a confession to that effect. On Monday morning, District Attorney Grant Bowen would file murder charges against David Blackwell.

Blackwell may have pled guilty, but some testimony was still required before sentencing could be handed down. Judge Taylor Wines heard all the testimony, and then did something no other Nevada judge had ever done after a guilty plea was entered; he disqualified himself from the penalty phase because he was morally opposed to the death penalty for minors. Judge Wines' feelings on the issue ran deep. Three years earlier, he and Oliver Custer were attorneys for Floyd Loveless in his Supreme Court appeal. Loveless lost the appeal and his bid for commutation.

When he was finally executed on September 29, 1944, seventeen year old Floyd Loveless became the youngest person ever executed by the state of Nevada.

Knowing this to be a death penalty case, Wines stepped down and assigned the case to Judge Merwyn Brown who took over for the penalty phase. In asking for first degree conviction and the death penalty Deputy District Attorney Bowen said that Blackwell had lain in wait for the two police officers with his gun set to go.

"Law enforcement in Nevada has become a serious problem due to the influx of hoodlums, and the officers are doing their best to meet that problem. The way to demonstrate to these hoodlums that they are not wanted here and the way to stand behind the officers is a verdict specifying the death penalty for Blackwell."

Blackwell's attorney disagreed. Blackwell, he argued, had not known that Geach and Glass were police officers. And there was no willful deliberation or premeditation. In closing, he said, "If we are going to lynch defendants I say dispense with the courthouse and hang them on a tree across the street."

Judge Brown believed that David Blackwell had shown reckless disregard for life on that November night. Further, the judge found the killings were willful, deliberate and cold blooded. That said, he sentenced Blackwell to die in the gas chamber.

It would not be a swift journey; while he waited on death row, Blackwell's attorneys asked the Nevada Supreme Court for a new trial. Ironically, they argued that David Blackwell had faced double jeopardy when Wines disqualified himself. His plea was denied. Blackwell turned to the U.S. Supreme Court who refused to review his murder conviction. Friday, April 22, 1949 was set as the date of execution.

Four days before his execution Blackwell's attorneys sought a commutation to life imprisonment. Blackwell's mother and father appeared as witnesses and told the state Pardons and Parole Board how David had always been a good boy until being sent to the Washington state reformatory. Next up were two pastors who had come to know Blackwell during his time at the prison. He regularly studied the scriptures, had found forgiveness and was a changed young man, a young man who might help others that were incarcerated, if he should be permitted to live, they said. Though he did not appear on Blackwell's' behalf, Warden Sheehy agreed with their assessments of David Blackwell.

Blackwell had convinced everyone but the Pardons and Parole Board; his sentence was not commuted. He would die at daybreak on the 22nd, as scheduled.

David Blackwell was led from the holding cell into the gas chamber, as the sun rose. Forty two witnesses, many of them law enforcement officers, crowded around the window to catch a glimpse of the young cop killer. Blackwell showed no emotion. He had spent the previous night nibbling on a fried chicken dinner, sipping three chocolate milkshakes, and praying with his pastor.

While the straps were adjusted Blackwell remained steady and calm, a changed person. One of those who shivered in the cold predawn was Gene Cowan who pressed forward for a closer look through the window. He was here to keep a promise.

When Blackwell shot and killed his friends Roy Geach and Alan Glass, Cowen had promised him that he would watch him die in the gas chamber someday. At last that day had finally come.

The straps that held the condemned man's arms and legs were quickly tightened, and the guards stepped out, leaving him alone in the chamber. Blackwell looked out at the witnesses who had come to witness his death. Recognition spread across his face when he saw Gene Cowan staring back at him through the glass.

The deadly pellets dropped; there was so little time left. He nodded at Cowen with a wry smile and a wink...

Unfilial: Brookey Lee West

How sharper than a serpent's tooth it is to have a thankless child... William Shakespeare

Christine Smith was one of those women. Early on she seemed destined to live a hard life on the seedy side of town. Still, no one could have guessed that she would end up stuffed in a garbage can in a Las Vegas storage unit. But she did. And she was placed there by her very own daughter, Brookey Lee West.

Like that of her mother, Brookey Lee West's childhood was anything but idyllic. Christine Smith had never been the loving parent she might have been. She was young and attractive. And she was too busy falling in and out of love to spend much time taking care of her two children, Brookey and Travis. By the time they were grown it was too late.

When she died at 68, Christine Smith was a helpless old woman suffering the effects of a life spent drinking and smoking heavily. Christine also had Alzheimer's. She was living in an apartment in Las Vegas and she was happy. She'd made peace with the past. Life was good. She had friends and her daughter came from San Jose to see her regularly. That's more than her son Travis did. She hadn't heard from him in a very long time. No one had.

In her youth, Christine had been a wild woman. Jealous of her married lover she confronted him in a Bakersfield bar, shooting to kill. She missed. The crime still meant a fourteen year stretch in the California women's Institute.

This left Brookey and her brother to fend for themselves. And fend they did, until Christine was released from prison after serving only two years. And like she always had, she picked up where she left off and continued dragging them along from one place to another. No child deserves such a mother. But then, no mother deserves a child that would stuff her into a 45 gallon drum, and leave her to die. Clearly Christine and Brookey were losers in the mother/daughter sweepstakes.

February 5, 2001. There was that horrid stench. The manager of the mini storage caught another whiff as he again walked past unit 317. Curious, he opened the cluttered unit and saw the large garbage drum with dark colored liquid oozing from it. He'd found the source of the smell. Certain that whatever it was, it was not good, the man called the police.

One of the crime scene analysts knew exactly what the odor meant. "The unmistakable smell of death," he called it.

A blood test confirmed that the contents of the drum human. And the death certainly wasn't a suicide. The manager checked his records and gave police the names of the two women who had rented the unit three years earlier: Christine

Smith and Brookey West. Foraging through the items in the storage unit police found a wallet and other items belonging to one of them.

The investigation turned up neighbors of Christine Smith who told the story of Christine and her daughter Brookey who worked in San Jose. One night without so much as a farewell, Christine packed up and went to stay with her son Travis in California. At least that's the story Brookey told. But the curious wondered why some of Christine's things were in the resident's dumpster.

It was starting to look like Brookey Lee West had killed her own mother. The mess in the garbage can was identified as having once been Christine Smith. Travis Smith hadn't been seen or heard from in years, how had Brookey taken their mother to him? Then too, it was none other than Brookey Lee West's fingerprints on the tape that had held the lid on the garbage can tight.

Four days after the discovery at the storage unit, Brookey Lee West was arrested for the murder of Christine Smith. It's not every day that anyone is accused of killing their own mother. Our society is fascinated with outlying monsters, and the media glommed onto the sensational story. Brookey insisted her mother had died of natural causes and not knowing what else to do she had stuff the body into the garbage can. But why had a plastic bag been wrapped around the dead woman's head? And why was Brookey Lee West still availing herself of *mom's* social security checks? Brookey Lee West remained a suspect in the June 1994 death of her ex-husband Howard Simon St. John.

West's trial began on July 3, 2001. Explanation might have worked. If only science wasn't able to look at maggots and blowflies that have a penchant for rotting flesh. In testimony a forensic entomologist contrasted the different type maggot or blowfly that would have been present if Christine Smith had been alive or dead when placed in the container. In spite of what Brookey Lee West insisted, he believed that Smith had been alive at the time.

On July 19, 2001, after two hours deliberation, the jury found Brookey Lee West guilty of first degree murder. In sentencing her to life without the possibility of parole, District Court Judge Donald Mosely said, "While I think everyone would agree putting someone's mother in a garbage can to bury her is bizarre, placing her in there conscious to suffocate her is not only bizarre, it's criminal. You are sentenced to life without the possibility of parole. That's all."

In 2003 she appealed her conviction to the Nevada Supreme Court. She lost the appeal. In 2012 she made an unsuccessful attempt to escape the Florence McClure Women's Correctional Center in Las Vegas. She resides there today.

.

PART TWO
IT' A CRIME

O.J. Simpson Wants his Stuff

December 5, 2008...Snow was piled two feet high in other parts of the country. But here at the tip of the Mojave Desert it was just another sunny day in Vegas. By 7AM a crowd started gathering outside the Clark County Regional Justice Center. Some held up a signs that read *Free O.J*... Whatever happened, it would be newsworthy. It always was with O.J. And it had been so ever since the day a cameraman in a helicopter focused in on the white Bronco as it sped down the freeway with police cars in pursuit. A star had fallen. Perverse it may be, but fallen stars are hot news.

People waited outside courtroom 15A to see whether or not they would win the raffle for one of the coveted 15 seats assigned for the public's use. With O. J. Simpson set to be sentenced most of the available seats had been given to news media and those connected with the case.

Tough cookie, the honorable Jackie Glass was presiding, no one expected Simpson to receive a short slap on the wrist stay at one of Nevada's prisons. Still the aging O.J. may have hoped...

Among those lucky enough to win a ticket were Fred and Kim Goldman, father and sister of Ron Goldman, the young man who was brutally murdered alongside Simpson's estranged wife Nicole. Denise Brown, Nicole Simpson's sister and. O.J. oldest daughter, his sister and brother in law.

The years had taken their toll. O.J. Simpson in prison garb and shackled, was far different from the handsome football hall of famer who hawked Hertz rental cars in television commercials circa 1970. Gone was the smiling defendant, declared not guilty of the 1995 brutal double murder that stunned the world. On this morning Simpson appeared to be a broken old man. Fighting back tears, he addressed the judge.

"Your Honor, I stand before you today sorry. Somewhat confused. I feel like apologetic to the people of the state of Nevada. I've been coming to Nevada since 1959. I worked summer jobs for my uncle in '60 and '61, and I've been coming ever since, and I've never gotten into any trouble. People have always been fine to me.

When I came here, I came for a wedding. I didn't come here to…I didn't come here to reclaim property. I was told it was here. When he told me that Monday, that stuff was in Nevada when he heard nobody was going to be in Nevada, I called my kids. I talked to my sisters, I called the Brown family and I told them I had a chance to get some of our property. Property that over the years we've seen being sold on the Internet. We've seen pictures of ours that were stolen from our home going into the tabloids.

We've called the police and ask them what to do. They've told us what to try to do, but you can never find out who was selling it, and this was the first time I had an opportunity to catch the guys red handed who had been stealing from my family. back.In no way did I mean to hurt anybody, to steal anything from anybody. I just wanted my personal things."

Judge Glass wasn't buying it. "When you take a gun with you and you take men with you in a show of force, that is not just a 'Hey, give me my stuff back.' That's something else and that's what happened here," she admonished him.

Before imposing sentence on the former football star, Judge Glass told those in the courtroom, "I'm not here to try and cause any retribution or any payback for anything else I want that to be perfectly clear to everyone."

At this writing Simpson has been released from Nevada's Lovelock prison and is reportedly living the good life in…Las Vegas.

Hanky Panky on the High Roller

The High Roller is one of Las Vegas's newest attractions. It dwarves others wheels like London's Eye, which is 443 feet tall, and Paris' Roue de Paris, (a mere 200 feet tall.) Only 9 feet taller than the Singapore Flyer, the High Roller at 550 feet tall, is the world's tallest observation wheel (Ferris wheel.) Adorned with 2000 LED lights that constantly change color, the High Roller at the LINQ is awe inspiring from every vantage point. When the High Roller's 28 glass enclosed capsules (cabins) are at capacity, there are 1120 taking the 30 minute ride. Brides looking for someplace unique to share their vows are already eyeing the High Roller. And so apparently, was one couple looking for a new twist on the old *mile high club.*

View from one capsule to another nearby capsule on the High Roller

On February 5, 2016 the adventuresome pair decided to undress and try a little hanky panky of the most serious sort while alone in one of the enclosed cabins. Ah, but there are those windows. And passengers in other capsules caught glimpses of the naughty duo doing the dirty.

You know what they say about cell phones being everywhere. Then too, there was that supervisor who used the intercom to tell them to and stop what they were doing and put their clothes back on. The calls were heedless. Police were called and when the high roller came to the docking area, the couple was escorted to jail.

Sadly, there is a rest-of -the-story to this story. The man involved in the sexcapade was recently murdered in his hometown of Houston, Texas. Apparently he fell victim to a carjacking turned deadly.

"The Dog House" - Reno, Nevada

Cheaters at the Dog House

The Dog House on Center Street in downtown Reno had it all: gambling, dancing, live entertainment and a restaurant. In the early days of legalized gambling (the 1930s-1940s,) it was one of Reno's most popular clubs. In the time before the Nevada Gaming Commission was created by Legislature in 1959, the task of maintaining gambling's integrity fell to local law enforcement.

On the night of July 5, 1939 Washoe County Sheriff's deputies walked into the Dog House and quietly watched the roulette wheel and its operators, George Coppersmith and George King.

Several hours passed. One gambler after another lost his bet. No one seemed to be winning but Coppersmith and King. The deputies didn't like these odds, and decided that the longtime gambling operators were cheating their customers by controlling the wheel with some sort of switch or mechanical device.

They confiscated the roulette wheel and arrested the two men who vehemently denied the charges. When deputies examined the roulette wheel later, they discovered an elaborate magnetic system built into the rim of the wheel. When a ball with a steel core was used the operator could control what section it dropped into.

The District Attorney revoked the Dog House's gambling license that covered ten slot machines, a 21 game, a roulette game and a craps game. The license was restored after owners proved that the crooked roulette wheel was being operated without their knowledge.

The day before they were scheduled to go to trial, Coppersmith and King pleaded guilty to operating an electrically controlled roulette wheel. Each was fined $1000. In addition to his fine, King was sentenced to six months in the county jail because he was listed as the owner of the game on a county license application. Neither man was ever involved with Reno gaming again.

The mob's rule in Las Vegas has ended. Today the Nevada Gaming Control Board and Commission regulate the state's gaming with the most stringent of rules. In order to obtain a gaming license to own, or operate a casino, one must be squeaky clean and pass a thorough background check.

This ensures that only those with impeccable integrity are licensed as casino owners and general managers. In fact, everyone who works in the gaming industry, from the pit boss to the change person, is subject to a rigorous background check before obtaining the required *police card*. Without which, employment in the gaming industry is impossible. A valid police card is required at all times while one is working on the floor. Like drivers' licenses, these cards expire regularly and must be renewed.

The gaming commission also maintains what is referred to as *The Black Book,* a list of undesirables who are not permitted entrance to any gambling establishment at any time in the State of Nevada. It was this inattention to detail that cost singer Frank Sinatra his gaming license at the Cal-Neva Lodge at Crystal Bay in 1962 when he permitted mobster Sam Giancana to openly stay at the Cal-Neva.

Suffer for Beauty

Everyone in Vegas is trying to make a buck. Some do it the honest way by punching a clock at one of the hotel/resorts, or working at any other of thousands of jobs. Some want to cut corners and make their money fast without worrying about such legalities as licenses. Such was the case of Ruben Matallana-Galvas and his wife Carmen Torres-Sanchez who set up their unlicensed cosmetic surgery center in the back of a Las Vegas tile store. To gather customers for their cosmetic procedures Matallana-Galvas and Torres-Sanchez were advertising in local beauty salons. It worked.

Here in the land of the skimpiest of the skimpy bikinis, youth and beauty are valued above everything else. Beauty and youth are essential to one's getting ahead, without it, you can forget it. The French have a saying "Il faut souffrir pour etre belle." Which translates that one must *suffer* to be *beautiful.*

Waxing eyebrows is one thing, but what happens when the suffering becomes deadly as it did in the case of forty-two year old Elena Caro?

Caro only wanted a more rounded and youthful backside. To perform her butt enhancement, Caro chose the cosmetic surgery center of Ruben Matallana-Galvas and his wife Carmen Torres-Sanchez. Everyone wants to be beautiful. Not everyone can afford the high price of beauty. Seeking something reasonably priced, Caro had first met the pair when she decided on having facial injections. The work was a cinch. She liked her smoother, younger face. Within a few days she was making arrangements to improve her *butt.*

On April 9, 2010 she arrived at the tile store for her scheduled appointment. She was given an anesthetic and injected with a gel like substance. Then something went terribly wrong. Elena Caro suffered a fatal allergic reaction to the anesthetic. Rather than call 911 for her, Matallana-Galvas and Torres-Sanchez made a run for it. Somehow Elena managed to walk out of the store. She made it to the corner of Pecos Road and Lake Mead Boulevard, where she begged passersby for help. An ambulance was summoned but Elena Caro was pronounced dead on arrival at the hospital.

Matallana-Galvas and Torres-Sanchez packed up cash and a few belongings and sped to McCarran International Airport where they purchased two one-way tickets back home to Colombia. They might have made it, if metro had been a bit slower. Luckily they weren't. They were nabbed at the boarding gate and taken to jail.

The pair pleaded guilty to involuntary manslaughter, conspiracy and practicing medicine without a license. In October they appeared before Clark County District Court Judge Abbi Silver and tearfully pleaded for leniency. Judge Silver wasn't buying it. They were each fined $12,000 and given the maximum sentence allowable of up to eight years in prison for their part in Elena Caro's death.

Downtown Bank Robbery

The take was over a million dollars, making it the largest bank robbery in US history at that time. And it took place during a parade in downtown Reno on Friday September 27th 1974. Everyone loved the Shriners parade this day was no exception. At 6:30 in the evening the noisy parade began marching its way down Reno's N. Virginia Street. As a cheering crowd gathered on the downtown sidewalks, a green van pulled up in the alley behind the largest bank in Reno, Nevada State Bank on the corner of Second Street and N. Virginia. Three men jumped out and ran for the door. While bank employees wrapped up their tasks for the day, the three men entered the building through a basement door.

The bank had been closed for nearly an hour. The only people in the building were employees. The bank operations officer, Bob Frantz and his assistant Mary Bennett started downstairs to close the safety deposit vault. As they reached the last step, one of the robbers grabbed Bennett roughly, pushing a gun into her ribs. Startled, she screamed.

"Shut up," He ordered. "Or I'll kill you!"

Bennett trembled in fear. Her assailant wasn't alone, behind him stood two other men. All three were similarly dressed in cheap Halloween masks, blue jumpsuits and rubber soled shoes. While Bennett was held with a gun pressed against her, one of the other robbers grabbed Frantz.

"You," he told Bennett, "Are going to walk up the stairs and over to the man on the phone and tell him what's happening and to hang up."

She nodded her understanding. As she approached the bank manager, Herb Brown's desk, he looked up from the phone, noticing the robbers.
"I'll call you back." He spoke into the receiver. The person on the other end of the phone kept talking. Brown listened silently.

"If you don't get off that goddamn phone I'm going to shoot her where she stands." One of the robbers snapped angrily. Brown hung up the phone. The robbers ordered one of the tellers to open the cash drawers, then led all the employees to the vault and handcuffed them. When their duffle bags were stuffed full, the three robbers raced out to their getaway van. An hour later the stolen vehicle was discovered in the parking garage at Sierra and Court Street, across the street from the Washoe County Sheriff's office.
The take was over a million dollars, and according to the FBI, the largest bank robbery in United States history at that time. Bank robbing is a federal offense; FBI agents converged on the downtown bank, while they interviewed the bank's employees, and sifted through clues, police officers had their hands full with onlookers curious about what was going on in the bank.
In November Ed Malone, Curtis Ray Michelson and Floyd Clayton Forsberg were arrested by the FBI at a private residence in Newport Beach California. Trial was set before Federal Judge Bruce Thompson at the federal court on Booth St, for June 2nd. Floyd Clayton Forsberg had other ideas. He and another inmate escaped from the jail by climbing out through a vent and placing a ladder across the roof of the jail to the Riverside Hotel/Casino.

Security was tight on the morning of the trial; a U.S. Marshal from Sacramento set up a weapon detector outside the courtroom. Anyone coming into the hallway or that area of the courtroom would be electronically scanned for metal; this procedure, though standard practice today, was set up as a precaution only for the duration of this trial.
With Forsberg still missing, Ed Malone, Curtis Ray Michelson appeared before Judge Thompson; Malone promptly pled guilty to the heist. He would be sentenced to 20 years for his part in the crime.
Michelson claimed his constitutional rights had been violated when FBI agents arrested him in Newport Beach; he wanted certain evidence suppressed. Judge Thompson ruled against him, the evidence would be presented. After a short trial, Michelson would walk away a free man after the jury voted to acquit him.
This left only Floyd Clayton Forsberg still at large. On the morning of June 29, 1975 Forsberg and his wife were holed up at the Riverside Motel in Bend, Oregon; in the adjoining room was the accomplice who had aided Forsberg's escape from the Reno jail. The three fugitives were sleeping soundly when at 3:30 in the morning the doors suddenly crashed open and FBI agents surrounded them.
Everyone was accounted for, except for 20 year old Denise Catlin, who was known to be traveling with Forsberg. The trio steadfastly denied any knowledge of the young woman's whereabouts. And the bank heist case took a strange turn.

In October a woman's body was discovered in a shallow grave near Bend, Oregon. Authorities believed she was the missing traveling companion of Forsberg. When her identity was positively established, they charged Forsberg with her murder; he pleaded innocent and a trial was set for July. In the meantime he was convicted of the Reno bank robbery in federal court.

Forsberg's erstwhile pal, Sam Fells took the stand and told the court how the three men had methodically planned the robbery. He was living in Sparks, and drove by the bank every day when he took his girlfriend to work downtown. One day he decided the bank would be an easy target.

"I just thought it could be robbed." He said. Then he went on to explain how he stopped in the bank to watch the habits of employees. "After a period of time I told Michelson about it."

In April of 1974 he shared his plan to rob the bank with Floyd Clayton Forsberg and his wife, who were staying in Las Vegas. But how had the robbers entered the bank so easily? With a key, of course; Fells told the court that he and Sorgre went to the bank months before the robbery to make a key. While Sorgre acted as lookout, he removed the lock from the bank door they would enter and replaced it with another lock.

"It took about three to five minutes--no longer than five minutes."
He took the bank's lock to a motel room, made a key for it, then took the lock back to the bank and replaced it.

"The bank's lock was old, some of the tumblers fell out and I had to replace them."

A few days before the robbery he went back to the bank to make sure the lock hadn't been replaced. He and Forsberg then went to Sacramento where they stole a green State of California van to use as their getaway vehicle. Back in Reno, they rented a small warehouse on Telegraph and stored the van and other robbery materials until they robbed the bank.

Next up was Pete Weems who testified how he helped Forsberg escape from Washoe County Jail; for his services, Wels was to be paid $20,000. After the escape, Forsberg, according to Wels, told him details about the robbery.

Forsberg was convicted of bank robbery. Before his scheduled murder trial date in Oregon, Forsberg changed his plea to guilty and was sentenced to life imprisonment at the Oregon State Prison. He was discharged in February 1994. His book *The Toughest Prison of All* was published in 2015.

Where's Bill Brennan and the Stardust's $500,000?

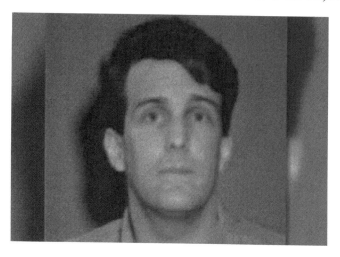

The Stardust opened in 1958 and operated 24/7 for the next forty-eight years. In that time the casino was robbed three times.

Like D.B. Cooper, he could be anywhere, the man who walked off shift with $500,000 of the Stardust's dollars never to be seen again. There are those who believe Bill Brennan had an accomplice who killed him, took the money and split. But that could just be wishful thinking on the part of those who like their casino robberies neatly solved. Perhaps Bill Brennan didn't get away. And he's not enjoying his ill-gotten gain on some island paradise. Maybe he's moldering in some lonely desert grave between Vegas and Stateline.

Brennan wasn't the first to help himself to Stardust cash. Royal Hopper beat him to that in September 1991. Hopper struck twice. The one million dollar take was double what Bill Brennan walked away with. But then Hopper got caught and Brennan hasn't...not yet anyway.

Both Hopper and Brennan were employees of the Stardust at the time of the robberies. Hopper worked two years as a security guard, sizing up the place and the money procedures, before making his move. Did I mention that he had the help of his son and a friend?

Did I also mention that Hopper, his two accomplices were arrested seven months after the robbery in April 1992? The robberies slid out of the news quickly. Casinos don't like to advertise their vulnerabilities. News travels fast in casinos. The employees knew. Bill Brennan was working in the sportsbook when Hopper committed his robberies. Maybe the robbery gave the thirty four year Brennan some ideas.

He'd been working at the Stardust four years. He was a good and trusted employee. This all changed on Tuesday September 22, 1992 when the good and trusted employee took a lunch break and walked out the door with $500,000 in cash and chips.

The investigation was handled swiftly and quietly. A half million dollars doesn't go as far as it once did. But it took Bill Brennan far enough away so that he was never seen or heard from again. The statute of limitations had long passed when the Stardust was imploded fifteen years later on March 13, 2007. Did Bill Brennan know? Did he even care?

Blast at the Orbit Inn Motel

January 6, 1967. Twenty-eight year old Richard James Parris wanted to end it all. Apparently he didn't want to go it alone, so the US Army deserter devised one of the most spectacular suicides Vegas has ever seen. He would have company when he exited this world. Parris arrived at the ultra-modern Orbit Inn downtown on the corner of 7th and Fremont with his 22 year old wife Christine, a gun and a plan.

Then too there were all those 50 sticks of dynamite. What was the motive? Was Mrs. Parris in on her husband's outlandish plan? Or was she just an innocent victim along for the blast into eternity?

Friends and family were shocked. According to his parents the marriage had been a happy one. Everyone agreed. Richard James Parris and his wife Christine were *so in love.* So why did he kill her, himself and four other people? He had deserted the army twice and had been AWOL from Fort Ord since November 1966.

Beyond that, there were no explanations, no answers to the question, why.

According to the Las Vegas Sun January 8, 1967 issue:

Deputy coroner Harvey Schnitzer reported the blast force was fantastic — scattering victims in an unbelievable manner. All of the victims were decapitated and one skull was found lying in an adjoining alley — it had been blown through the roof and over the wall. The leg of a woman was found embedded in a wall.

The newspaper went on to say that a woman's hand with wedding and engagement rings still on a finger was found. Six people (including Parris and his wife,) were killed in the blast that injured a dozen others.

PART THREE
WORST OF LUCK

Bring Me His Coffin

This is a strange story. First we have Arthur Velasquez and his wife, Thelma inviting friends to their apartment for drinks. As the party continued Arthur and Thelma began to argue with each other. After the friends left Arthur suddenly decided that Thelma needed to learn how to handle a gun. As an attractive coffee shop waitress, men noticed Thelma. This concerned Arthur. Just how a gun might help the lovely Thelma stave off the unwanted attention of other men, Arthur never said.

The gun of choice was a shotgun. So he went to the closet and brought out the family weapon. And that's when Arthur Velasquez' luck ran out.

He handed Thelma the gun. And while he expounded on the finer points of shooting, the gun went off, not once but twice. The wall of their South Virginia Street apartment was scarred with bullet holes and Arthur was dead…dead in his easy chair after uttering the words, "Oh my God sweetheart, you hit me."

At least this is what Thelma, as the only living witness, said.

. The story she told had her spending the next fifteen minutes in shock and anguish before calling for the help of a next door neighbor.

The neighbor called the police. And when they arrived, they thought this was no accident. Thelma was arrested and charged with murder in the second degree.

While she waited in the Washoe County Jail, a local mortuary prepared her husband's body for transport to Roseville California. As his widow, she wanted to say a final goodbye. Her attorney asked that she be allowed to attend Arthur's funeral and pay her last respects. Now imagine how well received she would have been to the dead man's next of kin. The DA demurred. Nothing doing. Thelma was beside herself with grief. Surely her attorney could do something. She needed to say good-bye to Arthur.

Shipment of the body was delayed until the matter could be resolved. Thelma's attorney turned to the Nevada Supreme Court. They sympathized but could find nothing in the law that would permit the widow to attend her husband's funeral. Finally, in what seems like an act of desperation, the attorney suggested that the coffin bearing her husband's body be brought to the Reno jail for one final visit.

While Thelma eagerly awaited word on the coffin's visit, jailers got nervous lest some weird precedent be set concerning visitors to the jail.

The Friday October 15, 1954 issue of The Nevada State Journal carried an article entitled, *There Will Be No Coffin In Sheriff's Office; Body Of Velasquez Is Sent Away*

The visit would not be permitted. The funeral home was free to transport the body to Roseville and the widow would have to say her farewell without gazing upon her husband.

But Thelma's luck was not entirely bad. She was being held without bail on a murder charge. However, the grand jury indicted her on manslaughter and her bail was set at $2500. Her friends put up the bail and she was out of jail in time to hang up her Christmas stocking.

While detectives continued going through Velasquez' personal effects, a strange letter was found. The letter, from a friend in West Virginia said in part...*How are things going with you? I have been worried. For several nights now I have dreamed about funerals in which you were playing a prominent part.*

Oddly, the letter was written and mailed just two days before Arthur Velasquez' death.

On May 2, 1955 Thelma was convicted of involuntary manslaughter and sentenced to one to five years in the state prison. When sentencing her, Judge Grant Bowen said he had thought about having her serve her term in the jail rather than the prison. But he decided against it because, in his words, "The county jail is no place for a woman."

How's that for luck?

Shoot First...Ask Questions Later

July 25, 1976. Friday night, she was home alone in her North Las Vegas apartment. Her longtime boyfriend had moved out weeks ago. Their constant fighting had driven him away.

She was tired....and just getting ready to call it a night. She worked at the Tropicana as a hotel maid. While others saw the glamourous side of *the Trop*, she saw another side. Her job was hard and grueling, an endless array of dirty sheets and towels, half used bars of soap and bathrooms that were unimaginably filthy. There was no glamour in her work.

Just as she reached to turn the bedroom light off, she heard someone at her front door. Startled she listened. Whoever it was started kicking the door in.

She grabbed her pistol from the nightstand and ran toward the hallway where she encountered a man. Not waiting for him to harm her, she raised the gun and fired once. That stopped him. He stumbled backwards and…that's when she realized she'd just shot her boyfriend.

Crying hysterically, she called the police. Everything checked out as she said. She was lucky. No charges would be filed against her. The boyfriend however, was not so lucky. He was dead.

Les Cole's losing Hand

The best laid schemes of mice and men
Go often askew,
And leave us nothing but grief and pain,
For promised joy!

When it was all said and done Les Cole might have agreed with Robert Burns in his *To a Mouse*. No one saw their *best laid schemes* crash and burn the way Les Cole saw his do so. But then, nothing good ever comes of plotting murder.

Les Cole was one of those people who liked living in a small town. Not much action, that was fine by him. He ran his bar over at Gold Point and enjoyed his friendships, especially that of John and Morrella Karlheim who lived in the nearby nowhere town of Goldfield. Occasionally Les ate dinner at the Karlheim home followed by an evening of cards and drinks. He had the Karlheims by twenty years, but that didn't seem to matter, neither did the fact that Les and Morrella had known each other since her chanteuse days up in Ely.

Town gossip being what it was, some whispered that Les and Morrella had once shared a passionate romance. True or not, it was twenty years behind them. Back then Morrella had been stunning. At forty-nine, she was still an attractive woman who kept herself dressed in the height of circa 1950s fashion. Morrella was no slouch; her blonde hair was always stylishly cut, curled and coiffed.

It wasn't her good looks that attracted Les Cole so much as it was cold hard cash. That monthly two hundred dollars she received from a former husband was something to drool over. A lot of money in 1951, it sparked Cole's greed. With that cash two people could live quite comfortably. But there was the problem of her husband John, the third wheel in Les Cole's scheme.

Once Les convinced Morrella to dump John and hook up with him, they'd be living the good life. But how best to achieve the departure of John Karlheim?

In Ely Les encountered Morrella's former husband in the local bar one night. Emboldened by a few drinks, he asked the man, "What would you say if I cut in on John's time with Morrella?"

That love was history. The man had no interest in his ex-wife's love life. He looked at Les with a smirk. "I'd say that was Morrella's business and none of my concern."

That was the green light for Les. With the ex-husband not meddling he only had John to worry about.

Every time he and Morella were alone he reminded her that John Karlheim was a drunk, and that she deserved better. Morella agreed. She even promised to seek a divorce. Emboldened, Les drove her to Tonopah to hire an attorney. At the last minute Morella changed her mind.

Les shared his sob story with the local bartender that night.

"I wish I had her instead of John. We could be happy together and comfortable too. She gets two hundred a month from an ex in Ely. We could be mighty comfortable on that."

The bartender nodded in commiseration. Les' story was not the first such tale she had heard in her years tending bar. She would remember every word he said.

On Saturday night July 7th Les saw his chance to rid Morella of John. On his way to Tonopah he stopped in at the Karlheim's place. "Things are getting bad." He told them. "There's nothing around here. I'm moving on to Beatty where there's business at least."

"I was about to fix fried chicken." Morella said, wiping her hands on her hips. "Why don't you come by when you get back from Tonopah and have dinner with us?"

"Yes why don't you?" John agreed.

Cole accepted the dinner invitation and drove on to Tonopah. When he returned to the Karlheim home around eight he handed Morella a bottle of gin and the three of them sat down to their chicken dinner. Afterwards Morella cleared the dishes and mixed the gin with powdered lemon drink. They drank the concoction and played pinochle until late into the evening, friends enjoying one another's company.

It was after midnight when John suggested that Les spend the night rather than drive home to Beatty. Les admitted he was tired. He'd already driven to Tonopah and back. He readily accepted the Karlheims' hospitality. While Morella put clean sheets on the bed in the guest room the two men discussed the carpentry John was to do for Les. John poured himself another drink and gulped it down. He was well on his way to becoming drunk and oblivious.

Les had waited all night to put his plan into action. With Morella busy in the other room, now seemed like the perfect time. He slipped the small bottle of cyanide from his pocket and stealthily dumped its contents into the other man's glass. Unsuspecting, John took another gulp from the glass and placed it back on the table. Problem solved. But something went terribly wrong.

Abandoned Karlheim house where Les Cole mixed the fatal cocktail.

Something Les Cole could never have foreseen; at that moment Morella walked into the room, picked up John's glass and drained it. Les was stunned silent.

John stumbled into the bedroom. "Someone poisoned my drink." He moaned.

With his heart pounding furiously, Les wondered if he could save Morella. Was there an antidote? He searched frantically through the kitchen cabinets. While he did so, Morella dropped to the living room floor, as dead as her husband in the next room. His plans in ruins, Les realized there was nothing to do but play the hand fate had dealt him. With any luck he could cover up the truth.

The first thing he would do was call for help. When the switchboard operator answered the call Les screamed into the phone. "This is Les Cole. Get a doctor over here. Tell him to hurry. Morella's slumped down on the couch and Johnny's clear out…Hurry I think they're poisoned."

Later toxicology reports would confirm that both Karlheims had died of cyanide poisoning around 2 A.M.

No one else had been in the home but Les Cole. And his story changed every time he told it.

Courtroom of Esmerelda County Courthouse where Les Cole stood trial

Making matters worse were the memories of the people he had talked to about his feelings for Morella. After Morella's former husband told that Les had wanted to take her from John, the lady bartender remembered how he had sobbed out his sad tale of woe to her one evening.

"There are plenty of others in this town who had reason to poison Johnny." Les insisted.

Sheriff Kitchen didn't believe him, neither did the D.A. As the evidence against him mounted, Les told several different versions of what had taken place on that Saturday night. He was indicted for the murder of John Karlheim in September and stood trial one month later.

The defense insisted Les was not the culprit. The jurors disagreed. It took them an hour and ten minutes to find him guilty of the Karlheim's murder. His sentence was life in prison. At sixty-five that may not have seemed like such a long stretch. Surely it was long enough for Lester Cole to contemplate how easily fate can wreak havoc with one's best laid schemes.

The Third Time is No Charm

Sunday September 2, 1962 Thirty one year old Richard L. Doebler was attempting to defy the odds by diving into the shimmering swimming pool from the balcony of his ultra-modern second floor apartment. Proud of his successful dive, he jumped out of the swimming pool, ran back up the stairs and stunned onlookers for a second time with another flawless swan dive.

As any gambler can tell you, luck can change in an instant. Instead of walking away the winner in his weird game of chance, Doebler stood poised on the balcony set to dive into the pool for the third time. This time his luck ran out. He miscalculated the distance and was killed instantly when he landed onto the cement of the pool area.

Knock on Any Door

Of all the doors that magazine salesman William John Aitken could have knocked on, he chose the wrong one on the morning of February 7, 1952. Aitken had his quota to make and bills to pay. So what if the police department had revoked his solicitor's permit; just because some people had complained about his heavy handed tactics. These whiners couldn't stand a little high pressure sales techniques?

Did they think it was easy out here? Blistered feet, dogs barking at you and doors slamming in your face were no fun. Peddling magazines was a lot harder than it looked. If he had to, he could always fall back on the old woe-is-me disabled war veteran story he told so well. Bullshit through and through. That he could tell it with a straight face was amazing; that they could believe it with a straight face, even more so.

The twenty five year old sauntered onto the street of his choice and surveyed the houses. Not bad. He could probably get a few of the wives who lived in these well-kept homes to pony up for a subscription or two.

At the front door of the first home on the block, he gently dropped his case and rang the doorbell. While he waited for the door to open, Stat went over his sales pitch again. Habit, he knew the words by heart, backwards and forward. He heard footsteps approaching the door and smiled. The big howdy grin he'd long ago learned worked best. The door swung open.

None other than Dallas Seevers, Superintendent of Reno PD's bureau of investigation stood on the other side of the threshold. Stat's big howdy grin vanished faster than ice cubes in the desert. Seevers was the very person who had revoked his solicitor's license twenty four hours earlier. Some days aren't worth crawling out of bed for; nothing to do but go quietly. And go he did; right to the city jail, where he was booked for soliciting without a permit.

A Fishy Tale

William Raggio (Bill) had a long and distinguished career in in the law and Nevada politics. He served in the Nevada State Senate from 1972 to 2011, longer than anyone else in Nevada history. He was also the Washoe County District Attorney from 1958 to 1970. Before that Raggio was Assistant County District Attorney from 1952 to 1958. This is the story of an early Reno case Raggio prosecuted in 1954.

How's the fishing? After answering the seemingly innocent question of a stranger, angler Howard Enos found himself in hot water. The more he floundered for a reasonable explanation, the more he realized he was on the hook.

It all started on May 23rd 1954, a perfect day for fishing. The sun was barely up; the weather was warm and calm. Enos gathered his gear and headed for Hunter Creek. His luck was usually good there. If not he would go to his secret spot on the Truckee. In a pinch Teglia's Pond could also be counted on to render a nice day's catch; though one had to pay for the pleasure.

His creel was nearly filled when a stranger wandered up to him, "How's the fishing?" He asked.

"It's great!" answered Enos. "The kids and I must have over a hundred fish in the home freezer."

The stranger's demeanor changed perceptively. "Don't you know that's a violation of the law?" He asked.

Enos admitted that he didn't. The stranger introduced himself as a game warden and placed Enos under arrest. He then asked if he might see Enos' freezer. The hapless fisherman agreed and took the man, who he now knew to be a game warden, to his home on Allen Street.

When Howard Enos opened his freezer it was evident he hadn't exaggerated the size of his cache. The game warden examined the evidence and painstakingly counted 192 trout. According to the law each fisherman was entitled to have in his possession no more than the day's limit of 15. Since there were two other fishermen in the home (Enos' young sons) the game warden reasoned that Enos was entitled to 45 trout, no more, no less. He confiscated 147 of the trout, revoked Enos fishing license on the spot and charged him with having more than the days' limit in his possession. He would see the fisherman in court.

The whole ordeal made Mrs. Enos' head swim. How could her husband have been such a braggart? She waited until the game warden left then calmly asked,

"Don't you remember that you got a lot of those trout in Teglia's Pond? We paid 90 cents a pound for them!"

Too late, he remembered. There was no limit on the amount of fish that could be caught in a private pond. In his haste to boast of his prowess with a pole, Enos had neglected to tell the stranger that some of the fish were easier caught than others. Everyone knew fishing in a private pond was akin to shooting fish in a barrel; easy!

His day in court came less than a month later on June 3, 1954. Enos pled not guilty and admitted that he had been fishing in Nevada since 1938. In that time he had always been under the impression that the day's limit of 15 applied only to a day's catch and not the amount in one's possession. "I believe a lot of other fishermen are doing the same thing I did."

The game warden testified that Enos had told him all the trout came from Hunter Creek or the Truckee River. Then Enos testified that some of the trout had actually come from Teglia's Pond. But a wave of forgetfulness swept over him when he was asked exactly how many of the fish had come from the private pond and how many had come from public waters.

During his summation Assistant District Attorney William J. Raggio said, "Whether the limit is wise or not, we are not to say. The purpose of the limit is to prevent wanton waste of fish and game. "

Enos' attorney closed by saying that the state had not proven beyond a reasonable doubt that the fisherman had more than a day's limit of game fish in his possession.

Justice of the Peace Laurence E. Layman saw it differently. He found Berns guilty as charged, fined him $50.00 and ordered his fishing license reinstated.

Perhaps the fine helped curb Howard Eos of his braggadocio.

.

It is easy to hate and it is difficult to love. This is how the whole scheme of things work. All good things are difficult to achieve; and bad things are very easy to get...Confucius

PART FOUR
SORDID LOVE

Blessed

He was born in Reno on the last day of January 1961. Anyone foretelling the next 30 years of Darren Mack's life might well have called him blessed. Born to a hardworking, close knit family that owned the Palace Jewelry and Loan in downtown Reno, baby Darren Roy Mack would grow up to be a good looking man with more than his share of charm.

The oldest son and the heir apparent; Mack would graduate Reno High School where he excelled at baseball. This allowed him to attend the University of Nevada Reno on a baseball scholarship.

Even those who seem to live a charmed life come up against fate. In 1986 Darren Mack was 25 years old when tragedy struck with the unexpected death of his father. Suddenly Darren Mack was thrust into the role of part owner of Reno's largest pawn shop.

There's no shortage of people down on their luck in a gambling town like Reno. Business was always good at Palace Jewelry and Loan. And Darren was becoming a very wealthy man. He also became a married man that year. Five years and two kids later, the marriage was over.

His next foray into matrimony came in 1995 when he wed Charla, a stunningly beautiful young woman who dreamed of becoming a movie star. She'd had a couple of roles and wanted more…and then she met Darren.

There was enough money for anything and everything she'd ever dreamed of. They purchased a million dollar plus home in the posh Franktown area of Carson City that was double the size of the average home. Not satisfied, they spent more money on upgrades than an average home in the Reno area cost. Then they settled into a lavish lifestyle.

Theirs was also a sexually open relationship that included regular outings to Fantasy Girls a local strip club, and membership in Reno swingers clubs.

Motherhood changed Charla. After their daughter was born she slowly pulled back from the swinging and the strip club scene. She wanted to devote time to her child. Darren didn't like this new Charla. Their arguments were heated and vicious. If Charla didn't want to swing with him, he would seek sexual gratification elsewhere.

Nothing lasts forever. Charla's happiness crumbled. Darren was a bodybuilder. He spent long hours in front of the mirror pumping iron and posing. When he wasn't working out he was chasing other women. The marriage started to fall apart. Each blamed the other. Disillusioned Darren moved out. There was nothing more for Charla to do but file for a divorce. She did so on February 7, 2005. Darren was not going to let their split be anything but rancorous. He demanded she return the expensive jewelry he had given her during their marriage, claiming it was only on loan from the pawn shop. She refused.

As part of the family court divorce settlement Judge Chuck Weller told the Macks to work out an equitable financial settlement. There was so much bitterness between them they could not do this. Charla had no money to call her own. She needed a home for herself and their child. She would also need a car. Weller ordered Mack to pay her a settlement of $480,000 dollars so that she could purchase the home and car. In addition to that Mack was ordered to pay $849.00 monthly child support and $10,000 a month spousal support to his ex-wife for the next five years. A lot of money, but then again Darren Mack made a lot of money. His ex-wife didn't. Used to things going his way, Darren Mack was not pleased with these rulings. He was furious at Charla and Judge Chuck Weller.

On the morning on June 12, 2006 Charla brought their eight year old daughter to Mack's condo for her scheduled visit. A friend of Mack's took the little girl into the condo to watch TV while her parents talked.

Charla had seen Darren's anger and his rage. She was afraid of him and was well aware of what he was capable of doing to her. But on this morning he somehow lured her into the garage. And while their daughter watched television upstairs with the friend, Darren Mack cruelly stabbed his ex-wife to death.

The friend was alerted when he heard his dog whining downstairs. The dog crept up the stairs and wandered into the room covered in blood, he realized something terrible had happened. Shielding the child, he took her and fled the house.

Darren Mack's rage was not yet sated. He drove downtown to the family court and took up a good vantage point in the Galleria Parking Garage on Sierra St. across from Chuck Weller's office. Carefully taking aim, he fired the high power rifle. He was a good shot. The bullet went hurling through the window of Judge Weller's office hitting its mark. Luckily the judge would survive.

As Darren Mack fled the city, his friend called the police. They needed to check the welfare of Charla Mack. It was soon apparent that Mack had committed both crimes.

While police shut down and searched the airport Darren Mack drove to Mexico. While hiding out there he contacted Washoe County District Attorney Dick Gammick who also happened to be a very good friend of his. After a brief email exchange Gammick was able to persuade Darren Mack to surrender.

There was all the local pretrial publicity and his having tried to kill a judge. But it was Mack's longstanding friendship with the District Attorney, Dick Gammick that caused the DA to recuse his office from trying Mack.

Darren Mack's trial would be held at the other end of the state in Las Vegas (Clark County.) On November 5, 2007 just before he was to go to trial, Mack entered a guilty plea for the murder of Charla and an Alford plea on the attempted murder of Judge Weller. An Alford plea in one in which a defendant does not admit guilt but agrees that the evidence is enough to persuade a judge and jury of guilt.

He was given life for the murder of Charla and forty years for the attempted murder of Judge Weller. He will be eligible for parole in sixteen years.

Mack appealed to the Nevada Supreme Court in 2010, but the appeal was denied. He remains at the Lovelock Correctional Center in Lovelock Nevada.

Suicide by Plane

Contractor John Covarrubias was well-liked by his employees. To them he was an honest, fair and friendly man. He may have been all these things. But John Covarrubias was not a happy man. He and his ex-wife Nellie had been divorced for six months and he wanted her back. Around 11 PM on April 10, 1965 he went to her crowded bar the Branding Iron Bar in nearby Pittman (Henderson) to talk her into getting back together with him. Surely she would agree this time. But like she always did, she refused his overtures. No matter what he did or said, they were finished.

"You don't have long to live." He screamed at her. "I'll fly my plane into this bar and kill you!"

He turned to two men who were sitting at the bar. "She doesn't have long to live." He said.

They'd heard husband and wife arguments before and didn't take the threat seriously. Neither did Nellie…she should have.

She walked away from him and John Covarrubias angrily stormed out of the bar.

A light rain was falling as the bright green Cessna 210 twin engine taxied down the runway at Las Vegas McCarran Field. Covarrubias piloted his plane across the Phoenix Highway (Boulder Highway) flying low. A witness estimated the plane was only about three feet from the ground when it flew toward the bar and smashed into the parking lot.

Witnesses described it as *a Kamikaze sort of thing.*

"He was aiming for the bar." Clark County Sheriff's Lieutenant Bill Witte told newspaper writers. "The only thing that stopped him were the cars."

The crash left a thirty foot hole in the building. People ran screaming from the bar. Many of them were injured by the falling debris. One was severely burned in the plane's gasoline explosion. The only death was that of John Covarrubias. He was thrown from the cockpit on top of a burning car.

A year later Nellie Covarrubias was sued in District Court by twelve people who claimed their automobiles were injured in the crash.

Three years later another man facing divorce decided to end his life in a similar manner. August 2nd 1968. The Shaws had been married three weeks when Mrs.

Shaw filed for divorce. This depressed Everett Wayne Shaw who thought the marriage would last forever. The airplane mechanic stole a Cessna 180 from the airfield in Jean and flew toward Las Vegas. He was set to end it all at the new Landmark tower which was 297 feet tall (at that time the tallest building in Nevada.)

Apparently Shaw changed his mind at the last minute and pulled up. Too late. The plane clipped the top of the tower and crashed into the Las Vegas Convention Center across the street.

Everett Wayne Shaw was the only person to die in the plane crash. He had thoughtfully left suicide notes in both his apartment and that of his ex-wife.

Thelma's in the Trunk

There's a problem when marriage suits one partner and not the other. Eugene Gambetta liked being married. His wife Thelma didn't. She'd been married twice before and wasn't averse to making changes. But Gambetta couldn't, or wouldn't, see her unhappiness. When she filed for divorce he blamed her sister Lola. If not for her influence he was certain Thelma would never have run off and left him. Under Lola's direction she not only filed for divorce, she refused to talk with him.

They were the happiest couple in San Francisco when they exchanged wedding vows in 1945. Like all newlyweds they planned for the future, seeing nothing but happiness ahead of them. He was a bartender. She was a waitress, and pretty. Men noticed her. And this gave rise to Gambetta's jealousy.

Three years after saying, "I do," Thelma Gambetta was ready to call it quits. When her sister offered to share her apartment in Reno with her Thelma packed up and eagerly headed for Nevada and a new life. But Gambetta wasn't about to let go so easily.

After the required six weeks, Thelma had her divorce and a job in a downtown club. The dark haired beauty took back her maiden name Thelma Ribail, and

began working as a shill, luring would-be gamblers to part with their cash in hopes of hitting a lucky streak. Good work, decent pay; Thelma was making friends and meeting new people. Most were men. She was young and single; late night drinks and dancing became part of her after work Reno routine.

Gambetta didn't like it; she was still his. After several heated phone conversations, he realized there was only one thing to do. Drive to Reno and beg her to come home. Nothing doing; Thelma was enjoying her new carefree life too much to ever return to his tight-reined jealousy. But she underestimated just how far her ex-husband's would go to get her back. Her older sister Lola was more observant. She saw what Thelma couldn't. Gambetta was a dangerous man.

Fearing that he might try to kidnap Thelma, her sister devised a plan. If Gambetta should ever force Thelma to go with him she was to leave her shoes and her hat as a sign that he had taken her. Neither woman probably thought they were being anything more than careful. And then the unthinkable happened.

Gambetta decided to try and make Thelma see reason one last time. He dialed the number and waited. Lola answered. No, Thelma wasn't home. She explained that her sister was working the late shift and hung up on it. He hadn't come all the way from San Francisco to be lied to again. He was tired of her lies. And he was tired of Thelma refusing to see him. He drove to the Gibson Apartments on West Second and parked down the block. Eventually Thelma would have to leave the building.

It was nearing dawn when a Buick rolled up to the front of the apartment building. A man stepped from the driver's door as Thelma eased out of the passenger side. So that's how it was. Gambetta watched them caress and kiss each other, his temper igniting. He jumped from his car and ran to the couple.

"Get away from my wife, mister!" He snarled.

Thelma's date was stunned. "Your wife?"

"I'm not your wife, Eugene. We're divorced!"

Ignoring her, Gambetta turned on the man. "Beat it if you know what's good for you."

The man stood his ground. "I'm not going anywhere."

"It's okay, Frank. I can handle this." Thelma assured him, sealing her fate.

He glared at Gambetta and got back in his car. "You sure?"

"Yes I'm fine."

He pulled the car from the curb; Thelma obviously knew the man and wasn't afraid of him.

Alone with Thelma, Gambetta pushed the pistol into her ribs and demanded, "Get in the car."

"I'm tired, Eugene." She moaned. "Can't we talk about this later?"

"Now!"

He hit her in the face with the gun. Dazed, she pulled off her pumps and hat and tossed them to the curb. A clue for Lola who would realize she had been kidnapped by her ex-husband.

He shoved her into the car drove toward Fourth Street. "I want you to come back to Frisco with me."

"I can't do that." She said.

"Does Lola have you hooked on drugs?"

"Of course not."

"Then why can't you come home with me?" He asked.

"I don't love you anymore Eugene."

Hurtful words, she couldn't take them back even if she wanted to. But she had to make him understand that it was over.

They were on the corner of Sutro when she tried to jump out of the car.

"You try that again and I'll kill you."

Thelma knew him and he was no killer. She grabbed the door handle again and swung to jump. He slammed on the brakes and fired, hitting her in the back.

He reached for her. No pulse. She was dead. And there was nothing left in the world for him. He turned the car around and headed west toward the Sierra.

There in the mountains overlooking Donner Lake, he pulled Thelma's lifeless body from the front seat and put her in the trunk.

She was going to Frisco with him after all.

He readily confessed when police surrounded his car the next day in a San Francisco park. Thelma's body was still in the trunk.

"Poor Thelma, I loved her so much…But I just got mad."

So did the jury. Eugene Leo Gambetta was found guilty of first degree murder in 1948 and executed at the Nevada State Prison in Carson City on October 18, 1949.

50th Birthday

W.S. Gilbert said, "it's love that makes the World go round." And that's true for most people. But not people like John Matthus Watson 111.

Everilda (Evie) Watson happily celebrated a milestone…her 50th birthday was on July 9, 2006. And her husband John threw her a surprise birthday. He'd also made arrangements to continue the celebration in Las Vegas. She must have been thrilled at the prospect of spending some time in Vegas, after which she would fly to visit relatives in Guatemala.

Little did she know, her husband had been planning her murder for nearly a month. Watson had complained to a friend that he believed Evie was thinking about divorcing him and taking half their assets with her when she left. That he said made him mad enough to kill her. Most damning of all, he told his friend that he knew places where he could hide her body and it would never be found.

He'd scrimped and saved for decades. Between his teacher's salary and her cafeteria worker pay they'd raised three kids, and somehow managed to squirrel away a nice little million dollar nest egg.

That wasn't exactly chump change. He would stop her at any cost. On July 10th he drove ahead to Las Vegas and rented a room for at the Circus Circus using his real name. Then wearing a disguise and using the name Joe Nunez, he checked into the two rooms at the Tuscany Suites he'd booked a month earlier. The second room he said was for Sal Nunez.

In booking the rooms, Watson had been very specific about which ones he wanted, 118 and 120. But Room 120 was taken so he chose Room 114 instead.

Evie's plane landed in Vegas the next day. An average looking woman making her way through the terminal and out into the intense desert heat, she may have allowed herself to smile as she thought of the fun she and John would have here. They'd been married over 20 years. She thought she knew him. She didn't. John Matthus Watson may have even smiled as he opened the door for her...Unsuspecting she stepped through the doorway. Everilda Watson would never be seen again.

A few days later Watson drove home to Ontario California without Evie. He explained her absence by saying she'd flown on to Guatemala where she planned to relocate. Evie, he said, had left behind credit cards, keys and her wedding ring. Alarmed, one of their sons filed a missing person report. Two days later Watson was arrested in the disappearance when it was discovered that he was carrying fake identification in the name of Joseph Ernest Nunez Jr.

The investigation into the disappearance of Everilda Watson continued with the discovery of blood in Watson's Jeep Grand Cherokee. He explained that Evie had cut her finger while opening a package.

Watson had no explanation for having purchased a band saw, odor neutralizer, incense, bleach, anti-freeze and odor absorbent bags the day he said she went missing. Neither could he explain Evie's blood that was in the carpet of that Tuscany hotel room, or her DNA in the shower drain of that room.

He was arrested and charged with the murder, kidnapping and robbery of Everilda Watson. He would confess to shooting her and cutting her body up with the saw. In a confession letter, Watson also told of cooking part of her body and eating it.

On June 10, 2010 after the jury found him guilty of first degree murder, Watson begged for the death penalty, saying he had converted to Islam and wanted to correct punishment for his crime. "You don't get to pick your punishment." The judge admonished him.

But somebody was listening. In the penalty phase of his trial, the jury came back and sentenced Watson to death for his crime.

Four years later he had a change of heart. He didn't want to die. Claiming numerous errors during his trial and the penalty phase, he appealed his conviction to the Nevada Supreme Court. The court found against him. The death penalty would remain.

I Love You, Walter...But what were You Thinking

Thelma Pinana probably did love her husband Walter Pinana. She just had a bad temper. A bad temper that turned Walter's good fortune fatal on the morning of September 14, 1958 when Thelma shot him to death with the revolver he had taught her how to use.

Wednesday January 28, 1959 was cold and cloudy in Reno. Dressed in a demure dark blue dress, Thelma Pinana was on trial for the murder of Walter Pinana, her husband of three weeks. Cliff Young and Leslie B. Gray. Accused of murdering Walter, her husband of three weeks, the pretty blonde glanced across the room at District Attorney Emile Gazelin and Deputy District Attorney William Raggio. The jurors looked at Thelma with curiosity. These twelve (ten men and two women) would decide her fate.

Three days into the trial, the bailiff announced that some jurors had been whispering and talking during testimony; this behavior, he explained, would no longer be tolerated. Judge Grant Bowen then excused one of them and replaced him with an alternate.

Among the witnesses called by the state were neighbors and acquaintances of the Pinanas'. lived in a small house directly behind the Pinanas. On the morning of September 14, 1959 she was visiting her in-laws, in the house next door to the Pinanas, when she heard what sounded like loud bangs and "a man's roar of pain."

She looked out and saw Walter stumbled out of his house and head toward the street. He was "bent over...holding his arms across his stomach. He was moaning."

Mrs. Lekton said, "I heard Thelma calling, 'Walter. Walter.' Then she screamed, 'I killed Walter' and ran out of the house."

The witness said that she had seen Walter lying in the street with Thelma kneeling beside him and crying, "Walter, I love you! Please don't leave me."

When she got no response from her husband, the witness testified that Thelma stood and said "I am going to torture myself." When a neighbor prevented her from going back into the house, Thelma dropped to the ground and beat her hands on the gravel.

Another neighbor testified that she remembered Thelma as "frantic and hysterical" on the morning Walter was shot.

Reno Detective Captain William Brodhead was called as the state's final witness. Brodhead testified that Thelma had admitted shooting her husband, but she couldn't remember how it happened. The Detective Captain said that when he asked her about the gun, Thelma said, "Somehow that thing got into my hand."

Brodhead said that Thelma was "crying and upset" when first taken into custody, but appeared "normal" later under questioning,

"I have one of those Irish German tempers. " Brodhead quoted Thelma.

When she was asked if Walter was mad, Thelma had told him, "Why yes, Walter was mad. Wouldn't you be mad if someone shot you?"

His testimony was devastating to the defendant who sat primly next to her attorneys and occasionally shook her head in disagreement. The final blow came when Brodhead told the jury that Thelma had been asked why she shot.

"Because I wanted to. You never know what's going on in a woman's mind."

Under cross examination Brodhead testified that when asked if she meant to kill Walter, Thelma had said, "No, I wouldn't hurt that boy."

Defense attorney Gray then asked Brodhead if he had advised the defendant of her civil rights.

Raggio objected.

Gray explained that he was referring to "her right to know that she was entitled to counsel…her right to refrain from making any statement."

Judge Bowen sustained Raggio's objection; "in a long line of cases," he ruled, "there is no such requirement."

Outside the Washoe County courthouse life and death went on. Jayne Mansfield was starring in *The Sheriff of Fracture Jaw* at the Midway Drive-In. *Around the World in 80 Days* was showing at the Tower Theater and *Tonka* was at the Majestic. Coins continued dropping into the hoppers of slot machines, Blackjack dealers kept pitching cards, Keno boards flashed twenty lucky numbers every ten minutes, and $1.65 bought a prime rib roast dinner at the Horseshoe.

Across the country, the rock and roll world of teenagers, and DJ's was shocked at the death of three of their own; Buddy Holly, Richie Valens and J.P. Richardson, the Big Bopper all perished in an Iowa plane crash enroute to a concert.

In District Court 2, William Brodhead stepped from the witness stand; the defense was ready with witnesses who testified to Thelma's early unhappy home of eight siblings and a father who drank. Subject to head injuries at an early age, she suffered from terrible headaches and blackouts.

It was nearly three o'clock in the afternoon. Thelma took the stand and began her testimony in a barely audible voice.

"Talk louder." Judge Bowen admonished her.

She stammered and wept as she told of two previous suicide attempts: once when she deliberately overdosed on her sister's medication, and again after arguing with her first husband. On this occasion she drank household ammonia. She also told how she suffered from severe dizzying headaches that "roar in my head."

While explaining how Walter taught her to use the .22 caliber revolver she said they saw a rabbit, "I seen it jump and I threw the gun to Walter and told him to kill it."

But she couldn't load the gun. "It wouldn't shoot. I asked him to come up and he said, 'you load it.' Then he came and looked and there was a live bullet in it." Thelma sobbed loudly. "He said he would have it fixed. "

Then she testified to the events leading up to Walter's death. As newlyweds, they wanted to celebrate their three weeks of marriage. "He kept telling me how pretty I looked…We never had a quarrel that I can recall." She said calmly. "I never ask Walter where he is going to take me, I just go with him. "

The evening began with them going out to dinner; she took only a few bites of her steak. "I just liked to see him eat so I gave him mine."

After dinner the conversation turned to the house Walter, who was a real estate salesman, wanted to buy for them. She suggested going to work. But he refused to let her take a job. "And that was that."

She told him her wedding ring was too big, and twirled it around on her slender finger in demonstration. Promising to get it fixed, Walter put the ring in his pocket. Then it was off to the 1091 Club on South Virginia Street for a night of drinking and socializing. As the evening wore on his mood turned sullen. Witnesses would later say that they argued over what he considered his wife's flirtatious behavior.

After a quick dance with her, Walter started talking politics with his friends. "I didn't want to back up there and hear him talk politics. There was nothing but men around there…Drinks started flowing from one to the other. I was feeling a little dizzy and sick and my head was hurting from not eating much."

Walter thought it would "be cute" if she danced with her friend Ricky* and so she had. "I've never seen Ricky with a girl." Later Ricky told her that Walter had left the bar. "I said, 'He'll be back.' "

And so he was. According to one witness, Thelma refused to leave when Walter was ready to call it a night; an argument ensued. It ended with Walter picking his wife up "by the waist" and pulling her out to the car. After the Pinanas left, the witness said he went to the bathroom and heard them arguing in the parking lot. According to Thelma she and Walter were not arguing on the drive home. They cuddled, with her arm around him and, "I kissed Walter like I always do."

When they arrived at their small house on Alvaro Street, Walter's mood changed. "If you want a divorce we'll do it. Then you can have Ricky or anyone you want." He said.

"I don't want Ricky!" She replied.

"Maybe I want a divorce." He said.

She raced into the next room, grabbed their marriage license and ran back to him. "There's your divorce." She shrieked, tearing the paper into pieces.

"I ought to make us some coffee." He said, suddenly calm. "Want a cup?"

Afraid that she would get sick, she nodded. "Call me when it's ready."

He left her alone in the bedroom; she stumbled against the nightstand, toppling the lamp. Thelma testified that when she reached to pick it up, "I started going backwards."

In doing so, she pulled the nightstand over; a drawer slid open. "I seen the gun…I thought I would try and unload it so I could show him next time we went out hunting I could do it so he'd be proud of me."

She took the gun to the bathroom. "As I remember him telling me you pull the trigger back and pull this other little thing…I heard him coming. I got scared he'd be mad because I had it...there was no place to hide it...he always told me it was dangerous and I had to realize it...I seen him standing at the door and he said, 'Oh my God, Thelma' and he went back on the bed and that's when I heard this noise and it could have very well been the bed I heard."

The packed courtroom was silent. All eyes were on her. Thelma hung her head and cried softly. Minutes passed; she composed herself and was able to continue. "Everything was awful quiet. I thought the gun had went off and hit him and hurt him."

She looked through the house for Walter and finally found him lying in Alvaro Street. "That look on his face it was...I can't describe it...I didn't want to live...I had hurt him and I wanted to kill myself."

Witnesses said she had sat in the street shrieking, "Walter! Don't leave me. I love you."

When the police and the ambulance came to take Walter to the hospital, Thelma wanted to go also. "I couldn't see why they wasn't taking me." Testifying about what happened once she was taken to the police station, Thelma said, "They put something hot on my hands. I thought I was at the hospital. "

She asked to see her husband. "I kept asking them to take me. They promised they would take me...Mr. Raggio said, 'You can stop lying now. Walter has already told us that he hit you and you shot him.' "I told him he was lying or that Walter was lying. Walter's not that kind of boy. He doesn't hit girls... Some policeman brought me two tablets. He said they would help my nerves. "

After she took the pills Raggio informed her that Walter was dead. "It didn't seem real to me. And it still doesn't."

Psychiatrist, Dr. Raymond M. Brown was called as a defense witness; before her trial, the doctor tested Thelma on three separate occasions. As a child, the pretty defendant had been beaten by a drunken father, and was the product of a broken home. She constantly found herself being accused of being sexually unfaithful and of "messing around."

Dr. Brown testified, "Here is a woman...sexually mistrusted early in her life...this is later reinforced in her first marriage...still later it is thrown at her...her security is threatened...it releases pent up feelings...raw emotions. A vulnerable part of her personality is her sexual actions and her security."

Under cross-examination Dr. Brown said, "...alcohol undoubtedly contributed to or aggravated this woman's condition...made her more vulnerable to this type of blowup."

During the psychiatrist's testimony the courtroom was so crowded that bailiffs had had to bring in extra folding chairs to accommodate the curious.

The doctor continued his testimony by saying that the defendant exhibited "extremely poor impulse control" and was an "emotionally unstable personality" who did not know what she did was wrong.

In his summation, Defense Attorney Cliff Young reminded jurors that D.A. Raggio had stated earlier, "I'll bet you" there was an argument in the couple's car enroute home from an all-night party.

"When you're dealing with human life you should not predicate human life and liberty on 'I'll bet.' It may be all right in the Nevada Club but in the second judicial district court we can ill afford such presumptions in dealing with human life."

Young also pointed out that defense psychiatrist Dr. Raymond Brown spent more time with Thelma than did Dr. Randolph Toller, the prosecution's psychiatrist witness; both agreed that Thelma Pinana was "emotionally unstable."

"Perhaps she was trying suicide. She's tried it before." He said. Regarding the premeditation charge he said, "Why did she just put it against his head...instead of waiting in ambush like Black Bart at Dry Gulch...as they contend?

"Temporary insanity is fully recognized as an excuse for a crime if it occurred at the time of the act even if the defendant were sane before and after the act."

He waved an arm at Thelma. "Her memory is not a whole lot worse than some prosecution witnesses...If she intended to kill why there is not some indication of an excuse? She could have devised something more credible than this."

District Attorney Gazelin rose to his feet. He looked old and tired; the trial seemed to have worn him down. Walking back and forth before the jury, he turned toward the defense and yelled, "Thelma knows what happened. Thelma Pinana told the truth to us on September 14th and 15th. And then she came to court and changed her story." He referred to Thelma and Walter's divorce argument on the day of the killing. "Thelma fixed that. She doesn't need a divorce."

Whirling around and pointing at the defendant, Gazelin said, "Thelma Pinana is the greatest violator. She violated Walter's right to live...There is only one person in this courtroom who can tell you what that motive is. She could tell you. Walter knew but Walter's buried. His lips have been sealed by her...It's a strange thing but many murderers are not people with past criminal experience...and that's exactly what Thelma is. "

Heavy wind pushed dark clouds across the Sierra and a light rain started to fall in Reno. At 4:30 in the afternoon the case was given to the jury. The ten men and two women deliberated Thelma's fate for the next seven hours. Snow was falling across the city when, at ten minutes to midnight, they sent word that they had reached a verdict. Solemn faced, they filed into the courtroom. Thelma watched them with interest, then lowered her head and listened intently as the foreman read the verdict.

"We find the defendant guilty of murder in the first degree."

The jury also recommended that she be given life imprisonment without the possibility of parole. On Monday Judge Grant Bowen sentenced Thelma Pinana to life imprisonment without the possibility of parole.

In 1960 the Nevada Supreme Court upheld her conviction and sentence of life without. Two years later the Pardons Board gave her clemency and commuted her sentence to life with the possibility of parole. In the fall of 1965 Thelma's name would again make news when Reno newspaperman, Rolland Melton broke a story about her having been transferred to the Lakes Crossing facility in Sparks; according to witnesses she was enjoying day passes and shopping trips in Reno, and had even been seen driving a car.

While at the facility and awaiting a hearing to determine his sanity to stand trial, a man accused of the brutal murder of a Supreme Court Justice, had also been issued day passes.

District Attorney William Raggio launched an investigation into the practice, calling for the names of all prison inmates who had been transferred to Lakes Crossing in the three years previous. Raggio also asked Governor Sawyer to investigate. Sawyer declined to comment on the matter. Nevada Health and Welfare Director, Wallace White conducted a full investigation of pass privileges and discovered that Thelma, who had been in residence at the facility for months, regularly enjoyed visits to Reno, dinner at a friend's house and visits with hospital employees both on and off the grounds. Her passes ranged in length up to 12 hours, but not overnight. It was 1965 and women at the facility were required to wear dresses; not Thelma Pinana. She wore slacks. She was also permitted to carry a purse and to receive visits from a friend who was a felon recently paroled for second degree murder. Apparently the two had met while incarcerated in Carson City.

Pinana's attorney jumped into fray by declaring that while he thought the passes were an error on the part of administrative authorities, he hoped no one would blame Thelma for accepting the passes given her.

White concluded his investigation and brought the practice of issuing passes to those from the state prison to a screeching halt; Thelma was returned to the prison in Carson City. She was awarded a parole in January 1968.

One Sided Love; The Murder of Kathy Augustine

People complain about politics as if it were a polite endeavor. But politics is a nasty business. There's always someone ready to sling mud at an opponent. One wrong move and allies can quickly become adversaries. Backstabbers are a constant. Kathy Augustine understood all this. She was savvy…and bright. Most of all she was tough. And for a brief time she thrived in Nevada's political arena.

In 1998 she became the first woman to serve as the Controller for the State of Nevada. She was re-elected to that office in 2002. Like all of us, she had her enemies...and she had her friends. Her husband of seventeen years, Charles Augustine died of a stroke in August 2003. The following month she went to Hawaii with William Charles "Chaz" Higgs a critical care nurse, eight years her junior, who had been involved in Charles Augustine's care. Higgs had all the right moves and all the right words. They married while staying on the islands. Friends were shocked at how fast the romance had progressed.

Kathy had nothing in common with her new husband, who stood alone and aloof at political events they attended. But there was no denying that she seemed so happy. That same year she was honored by being named the outstanding Italian-American of the year by the Augustus Society, a non-profit organization made up of Las Vegas men and women of Italian heritage. The feisty Republican seemed to be on a fast track toward political stardom.

In January 2004 she was advised that she was a finalist to become Treasurer of the United States. Augustine's hopes were high. Anna Escobedo Cabral got the nomination instead. And like a house of cards, it all started crashing down around Kathy Augustine.

She and Chaz were fighting more than ever. Their age difference was catching up with them. He was bored by her friends and colleagues in the political arena. When they attended functions, he was distant and sullen.

She thought he was cheating on her and sent him packing, only to relent and let him come back. She didn't want to be lonely. Former employees had complained about the work she'd forced them to do back in 2002 when she was running for re-election.

She was duly elected only to end up the only public official in Nevada (as yet,) to be impeached.

She could be the boss from hell. Screaming at and ordering her staff to work on her re-election campaign while on the Nevada state payroll clock. That's a big No-No. For this, Ms. Augustine faced the music and the camera with tears glistening in her eyes. Regardless their party affiliation, most people probably found it difficult not to feel some pity for the politician. That pity would soon turn to shock.

Not long after being impeached, Augustine was killed at her Reno home by her much younger pretty-boy husband. As it turned out, Higgs liked to show off at the hospital. Before the murder, he'd stupidly bragged to co-workers that the best way to kill someone was by administering succinylcholine (sux for short) which is a powerful paralytic.

When Augustine arrived at the hospital, doctors thought she'd suffered a heart attack. And then some of Chaz's co-workers remembered his boast about succinylcholine. Augustine's urine samples were saved for further testing. The results were conclusive; Kathy Augustine was killed by a fatal dose of succinylcholine. It was a cruel and cunning murder for which Chaz Higgs was convicted. He is currently serving a very long and very well deserved stretch at the Nevada State Prison.

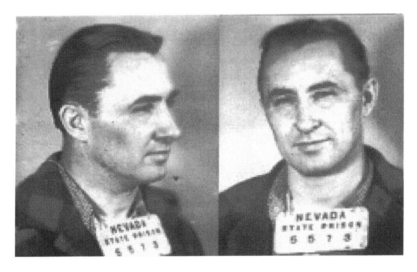

Theodore Gregory photo Courtesy of the Nevada State Library and Archives

She Won't Need a Doctor

Theodore Gregory was insanely jealous. His wife Margaret Tarr couldn't take it any longer and ended their two year marriage. They might be divorced, but Gregory was still in love with her, and would do anything to keep her. Summoning up all his powers of persuasion, he convinced the pretty brunette to give their relationship one last chance. He could change his ways, he promised. Things had soured for them in Las Vegas, sure. But if she believed in him they could make a fresh start in Reno. Life would be different, he swore to it.

Margaret wanted to believe him. A new start in Reno sounded like just what they needed. So they made up, packed up and headed for Reno. All they needed was a new place to call home.

With three children to feed and an ex-husband in Colorado, Margaret Tarr only wanted to get on with her life. Gregory just wanted her. So they moved into the same boarding house; there they lived together, but separately. That was the way she wanted it. And he readily agreed.

Money wasn't a problem. Gregory brought home a decent wage as a barber and Margaret worked as a night shift cashier at Harold's Club downtown. Outgoing and friendly, she quickly formed many friendships at work. Gregory couldn't understand it. Where he barely took the time to remember the names of the men he worked with, Margaret delighted in getting to know her co-workers.

When Margaret start staying after work with her new friends Gregory's jealousy resurfaced. All they did was argue. She wasn't his wife. He didn't own her. And she reminded him of that. He countered with one chilling threat: if he couldn't have her, no man would. Margaret laughed the threat off. He was jealous, but she didn't think he was dangerous.

He snapped on the morning of September 18, 1948. Seething with anger, he waited up for her all night long.

"I guess I lost her. She double-crossed me, I found out where she was that night, and I know what I'm going to do." Gregory told his landlady Mrs. Engelberger at daybreak as a car pulled up in front of the house.

He peered out the window. The car was that of Margaret's supervisor, a kind man who sometimes gave Margaret a ride home. By doing so on this morning, he had unwittingly put himself in danger.

Gregory stormed out the front door just as Margaret stepped from the car. She smiled defiantly at him. *She wasn't his wife.* He raced toward her and slapped her so forcefully that it knocked her unconscious. Waving his gun at the unfortunate Frel, he shoved Margaret over and jumped into the car.

"Drive!"

"But she needs a doctor." The man protested.

"She won't need a doctor. I'm going to kill her. "

"Where? Where do you want to go?" Frel asked.

Gregory directed him to drive to a deserted area on the western edge of town.

"Stop here!" He commanded.

Margaret woke with a start. "Why you worthless--"

He silenced her by pointing the gun at her. "You been running around on me again and this time I'm going to kill you for it."

"No!" She screamed. "No I haven't. You've got to believe me." She begged.

"I told you in Vegas I wasn't going to put up with your running around anymore."

"But you're wrong honey." She said.

Back and forth, they argued for several minutes. Then Gregory calmly nodded to the other man, "I got no beef with you mister. Beat it!"

The frightened man did as he was told. He jumped from the car and ran panting, as fast as his legs would carry him. Suddenly he heard three shots fired one after the other. He didn't look back. She was in trouble and needed help. Somehow he had to summon help.

Gregory jumped out of the car and made his way back to his home on Imperial St. When she saw him, his landlady greeted him warmly and asked how he was doing.

"Mrs. Engelberger," he said. "I have done something really bad."

She smiled at him. He was such a good tenant; always polite, paid his rent on time, and never gave her any problems. "I doubt that Mr. Gregory."

The landlady changed her mind when the police cars started rolling up to the house an hour later.

As he was being led from the house in handcuffs, Gregory turned back to the shocked woman, "I told you I had done something bad."

Theodore Gregory was convicted of murder in the first degree within the year. Despite appeals and pleas from family, friends, and even his first wife, there would be no clemency for him. On January 29, 1951 he was executed in the gas chamber at the Nevada State Prison in Carson City.

George Tiaffay

For the record, there are no easy jobs in Nevada's casino industry. Some are harder than others. Serving cocktails in Las Vegas is one of those. But the money is good. Cocktail waitressing can provide one with up to a six figure income and better than average lifestyle. This is particularly true if a woman is pleasant, exceptionally pretty, and working in a topnotch place. Shauna Tiaffay was just such a young woman. She worked swing shift at the prestigious Palms. Maybe not the perfect shift for a young wife and mother, but swing shift is generally where the money is. Besides that, she loved her job and got along well with her co-workers.

But everyone knew that Shauna's life was her husband George and her daughter. George was a West Point grad and a Las Vegas firefighter and her daughter was an adorable little girl with the features of both her dark eyed dad and her blonde mom. Shauna was happy.

Five years into their marriage the rosy glow dimmed. Shauna had never realized just how mean and controlling her husband could be.

Their life was in turmoil. There was no peace…no solace in their home. With George's constant barrage of hateful demeaning words and the presence of a homeless man (Noel Stevens) doing odd jobs around their place, Shauna was uneasy. George seemed to be on friendly terms with the man, but there was something about him that unnerved her. Did some part of her sense the evilness that lay beneath the surface of their odd friendship?

Finally she could take no more. She rented her own apartment and moved out. She had no intentions of ever going back to the abusive marriage. But George didn't want the marriage to be over. Nor did he want a messy divorce.

September 29, 2012 Early Saturday morning and a full moon hung over Las Vegas. Those in the casino industry know how weird people can get during a full moon. Friday had been a long night. And Shauna was tired. She punched out at the Palm's timeclock at headed home. George had their daughter so she could sleep late.

She unlocked her apartment door and stepped in. Out of the shadows he came, startling her. She tried to fight, tried to escape. But she was no match for the claw hammer he viciously battered her with.

Several hours later George would discover Shauna's lifeless body when he brought their daughter home. Suspicion always falls on the spouse of a murder victim, unless they have a very strong alibi. And George did. The day before he had left his daughter with her grandmother and worked a 24 hour shift at the fire station.

The killing of Shauna Tiaffay was brutal and senseless. The city was on edge. When would he strike again? Two days after the murder, investigators got the tip that broke the case wide open.

A man called police to report that a friend had confessed to him for killing a woman with a hammer, and striking her so many times that he broke the hammer. The friend went by the street name of Greyhound. And he lived in a campsite on the edge of the city.

When investigators finally located him, Greyhound admitted his name was Noel Stevens. But, he swore, he knew nothing about Shauna Tiaffay's murder. Then how did he explain the dead woman's blood on pants they found at his campsite? Looking through Stevens' cell phone they found the name George. When asked, Stevens admitted George was his friend the firefighter. Investigators discovered the two of them had exchanged over 80 phone calls during the month of September.

George Tiaffay's involvement in the death of his wife was becoming clear. There was more damning evidence to come.

Most large businesses have some sort of video camera in use. Lowes did. And it was this surveillance tape that caught George Tiaffay and Noel Stevens buying claw hammers and knives five days before the murder. It was all over. Noel Stevens confessed. George, he said, paid him six hundred dollars to kill Shauna, with the promise of more.

George Tiaffay was arrested and it was every man for himself. With the promise that the death penalty would be off the table, Noel Stevens agreed to testify against George Tiaffay.

During his testimony, Stevens told how Shauna had asked "Why are you doing this," as he battered her with the hammer. When asked who told him to kill Shauna he answered. "George."

After fifteen hours of deliberation the jury found George Tiaffay guilty of first degree murder. His sentence was life without the possibility of parole.

Noel Stevens was given a minimum forty two years with the possibility of parole.

Till Death Do Us…

What are the odds? Las Vegas real estate magnate Ron Rudin was murdered in the same month (just days before Christmas) and in the same bedroom that his third wife Peggy had shot and killed herself in sixteen years earlier. Rudin had discovered her body. In doing so, he absently picked up the gun she'd used to kill herself. Although one of her distraught relatives would later accuse Rudin of killing her, Rudin was never charged with the death of Peggy Rudin that was ruled a suicide.

Rudin was devastated. Eventually he started dating again. And he continued to changed wives the way most men change socks. When he met Margaret he had four marriages behind him. By most standards that made him a poor choice for a husband. But then, Margaret also had four failed marriages in her past.

On September 11, 1987 they were married in one of the city's quickie wedding chapels. And Ron Rudin moved his bride into his home at 5113 Alpine Place. The arguments soon started. Rudin was self-absorbed, and not the faithful husband, his new wife had hoped for. He was a player…he was cheap and he liked his liquor. Still, there was all that money. If she could hang on and wait him out. The money, or a large chunk of it, would be hers.

A year after the marriage Rudin filed for divorce claiming incompatibility, and Margaret moved out. Several months later, she moved back in and managed to get him to withdraw the complaint. Anxious to know what he was doing at all times, Margaret installed listening devices in his office. Now, she would hear everything he said and to who he said it.

What she discovered, she didn't like. Ron had a girlfriend, also married. What if this woman should take her place?

Margaret wrote an anonymous letter to the woman's daughter. This letter would later be presented as evidence in the prosecution's case against Margaret Rudin.

Your mother has been screwing Ronald Rudin the realter (sic) *for over a year. She meets him at vacant houses he owns during her work time…and she screws him on dirty carpet floors. He brags to his friends and laughs at her because he tells everyone he does not get a motel and he does not have to buy her a lunch.*

A divorce would be financially devastating. Ron had to die. He collected guns. The house was a virtual arsenal. She shot him in the same bedroom they'd slept together in as husband and wife. When he was dead she decapitated him, and drove his body out to secluded Eldorado Canyon and set it afire….

Ron Rudin was missing. One day he was there. And the next he wasn't. His anxious employees couldn't imagine their workaholic boss not showing up for work on time. They called his home only to receive the answering machine. When they finally made contact with Margaret, she seemed unconcerned. She didn't know where he was. Two days would pass before they convinced her to file a missing person's report.

Within a month a skull was discovered by campers. Nearby were a burned body and a diamond bracelet bearing the name *Ron*.

Ronald Rudin was no longer missing. Margaret Rudin claimed to know nothing. Detectives didn't believe her. When forensic investigators came to the house on Alpine in search of evidence, they found plenty. Not only were Rudin's tissue and blood spatter on the master bedroom ceiling but so were Peggy's, after all those years.

Margaret Rudin was charged in the death of Ronald Rudin. And although she maintained her innocence, she fled the state to avoid standing trial. She would be on the run for over two years before they caught up with her in Massachusetts and brought her back to Las Vegas.

For the Love of Alice

This thing of darkness I acknowledge mine. There is nothing more confining than the prison we don't know we're in. William Shakespeare

With the discovery of gold ore at nearby Columbia Mountain, Goldfield quickly became Nevada's largest town. Nearly ten thousand people rushed to the gold camp, hoping to strike it rich. Among them was Patrick Columbus Casey who decided he wanted a married woman.

Of all the women in Goldfield, Casey had eyes only for Alice Mann. From the moment he met her, he couldn't get her out of his mind.

He lived in a small cabin only a few yards from the home of Alice and her husband. And as neighbors a friendship sprang up between Casey and the Manns. While he enjoyed the friendship, he secretly yearned for Alice. She was kind enough, but not the way he wanted her to be. If only she would return his affections. Alice was a happily married woman and told him so whenever he dropped a subtle hint about his feelings.

And then it seemed that luck might be with him. Out of work, Mr. Mann left for San Francisco and a job. Now that she was alone, Alice might be persuaded that he wasn't so bad after all. To his dismay, she continued to spurn his attempts to woo her. Worse, all her friendship was now dedicated toward Thomas and Lucy Heslip. And they kept Alice from him. On the morning of August 17, 1909 Casey cornered Alice and tried to explain his feelings. She was tired of his unwanted attention, and wanted nothing whatsoever to do with him. Chafing after another rebuke, Casey headed to the Turf Saloon to drink away his troubles. Half drunk, he asked the bartender a question. "If a man were to murder someone and then try to kill himself, do you suppose he could get off with being crazy?"

It was an odd question. And it was one the bartender couldn't answer. Casey then asked to borrow his gun. No way. The bartender wasn't about to loan a gun to a drunk man. Undeterred Casey stumbled out of the saloon and headed home to get his roommate's revolver. Alice was about to find out how serious he was at getting her attention. Lucy Heslip was about to find out why it wasn't wise to meddle in the affairs of others.

If she and her husband had stayed out of the way maybe Alice would have given him a chance. At the Heslip house Casey found Lucy Heslip sitting on the front porch with Alice and another woman. They barely acknowledged him. He stopped and stared at them. Then, taking aim at Alice, he fired his gun. The young woman cried out in agony as the bullet struck her in the leg. Lucy Heslip jumped up.

"What on earth are you doing?" She screamed at Casey.

He pointed the gun at her and pulled the trigger. The bullet struck her in the forehead, killing her instantly. But Casey wasn't through. He fired another bullet at Alice, turned and calmly walked away from the horror he had just brought to this little house on the corner of Hall and Fifth Streets. He didn't get very far. Realizing what Casey had just done a man jumped him and disarmed him. Casey angrily pulled a knife and stabbed his captor in the shoulder. A crowd gathered and started yelling "Lynch him. Lynch him."

Realizing the danger he was in, Casey demanded the Sheriff come and arrest him. All of Goldfield was outraged at the senseless crime. And talk of lynching mounted. To insure his safety Casey was whisked away to the Tonopah jail.

When informed of his wife's death Thomas Heslip was inconsolable. He walked into the Gold Dust Saloon and asked for a glass of water. At the back of the saloon he gulped the water, using it to wash down a fatal dose of cyanide poison. "I'm going to join my wife." He told those who helplessly watched him die.

The object of Casey's affection, Alice Mann would recover, but she would be disabled. On October 26 1909 Casey stood trial at the Esmeralda County Courthouse. He had shot and killed an unarmed woman and left another maimed for life. The jury showed him no sympathy. He was convicted and sentenced to hang. His case went to the Nevada Supreme Court who found no error with the lower court's decision.

On the morning of August 16, 1911 Patrick Columbus Casey strapped on his artificial leg and listened as Warden Baker read him the death warrant.

"I'm ready." Casey sighed, and accompanied by the warden, two guards and a clergyman, he slowly walked toward the gallows. It was two years to the day that Casey had shot Mrs. Lucy Heslip in the head while she sat on her front porch visiting with two friends. He mounted the thirteen steps and stood squarely over the trapdoor. Steadying himself, he looked around the room at those who had come to Carson City to witness his execution.

"Today good people I face you and one of the most disgraceful deaths known to civilization." He spoke for a few more minutes then said of his victim, "The dear lady, Mrs. Lucy Heslip whom I have been convicted of murdering, I hope to God she is in Heaven where I shall meet her, and before my God in Heaven, I had naught against that poor innocent woman. May she rest in peace forever."

Earth provides enough to satisfy every man's needs, but not every man's greed. Mahatma Gandhi

PART FIVE
IT'S A MOB THING

Bugsy Wants In

Hollywood restaurateur, publisher and gambler Billy Wilkerson kept busy watching his Las Vegas dream take shape in the form of a highbrow gambling establishment. Wilkerson ran a swank restaurant in Hollywood, and liked rubbing elbows with film stars. He had the idea of enticing Hollywood's elite to Las Vegas with fine dining and games of chance. All he had to do was built a classy enough place and they would travel that hundred miles across the desert. Classy, that's what Wilkerson wanted his establishment to be.

But he ran out of money.

Like Wilkerson, Siegel admired class. He was impressed with what he saw and suddenly he wanted what Wilkerson had. In true Bugsy fashion, he shoved Wilkerson out of his dream and into an agreement. A legal document was drawn up. Ever the gambler, Wilkerson figured the odds and gladly signed on the dotted line. After all, signing away his dream was better than taking up permanent residence in a six-foot plot of the Southern Nevada desert.

Benjamin "Bugsy" Siegel has been called the Father of Las Vegas. Deserved or not, it's not a bad thing to be known as, especially for a mobster.

Siegel started life in the New York slums, the son of poor immigrant parents on February 20, 1906. He and Meyer Lansky met as teenagers and a close lifelong friendship began.

When personnel problems erupted in Los Angeles, Meyer Lansky sent Siegel out to the west coast to straighten things out. Like thousands of others before him, the handsome Bugsy quickly became star struck and fell under the southern California spell with its sunshine, palm trees and movie stars.

The dashing man about town was just how Siegel envisioned himself. He belonged here. There would be no going back to the east coast, not with all that Hollywood had to offer.

While Siegel squired beautiful starlets, his wife and family waited for his return. To keep them near, he rented a spacious home in nearby Beverly Hills and moved the wife and kids in. Ever the debonair ladies' man, he wasn't about to let a little thing like a family stand in the way of his romantic pursuits with several well-known stars of the day. Occasionally he would head for a little rest and relaxation in the desert gambling town of Las Vegas, some 100 miles east.

Gambling had only been legalized in Nevada a few years; watching people happily engaged in the pursuit of winning, Bugsy was intrigued with how much of their money they were willing to risk at the tables, the roulette wheels and the slots. He may have only had an 8th grade education, but Bugsy was smart enough to figure the odds.

He was in town to take care of Lansky's horserace betting operation when he started to seriously consider the potential here in the desert. There was a tremendous amount of money to be made. And amazingly, it was all legal. The suckers couldn't wait to hand over their cash. They might have called it gambling, but Bugsy knew better. He was nobody's fool; the odds are always in the house's favor. Sooner or later, the house wins. Always!

There were a few gambling establishments like the El Rancho and the Last Frontier, but Las Vegas still lagged behind Reno as gambling's fun spot. The 40 year old city had seen its shot at fame come and go with the Boulder Dam Project. Now it needed a new direction. And Benjamin Siegel was just the man to see that it happened.

Wilkerson's dreams might be dashed, but Siegel's were taking shape. He would call the hotel the Flamingo after his long legged girlfriend Virginia Hill who had a penchant for colorful flamboyant attire. Under Bugsy's watchful eye work on the Flamingo hotel continued while his bosses back east waited for his gamble to pay off.

Everyone in town didn't agree with Siegel about the Flamingo. On August 1, 1946 The Las Vegas Tribune carried a front page editorial criticizing him for having the audacity to use scarce material in the building of a casino. According to the editorial, this material could be put to better use by building homes for returning war veterans. Especially since the Civilian Production Administration (CPA) was organized for the purpose of building homes rather than commercial establishments. But Bugsy was used to bending the rules, and none of this mattered; Whether or not he had used bribery as a means of securing them, Bugsy had obtained his building permits from the Civilian Production Administration and that was that; construction continued.

While Bugsy held tight to his bosses' purse strings, he was getting ripped off by unscrupulous the war had just ended and materials were difficult to come by. Anything that could be obtained was generally overpriced, and then there were the delays and the thefts. One rumor involves workers stealing material in the evening only to redeliver and recharge for it the next day. Bugsy, who would eventually pay with his life for the cost overruns, was none the wiser. He might have been an excellent gangster, but Siegel was no businessman. Worse he liked to spend money, especially on horses, dining, and squiring beautiful women.

After patiently waiting for him to stop his philandering, Bugsy's wife finally decided enough was enough and filed for divorce in Reno. This left Bugsy more time to party with Virginia Hill was beautiful and vivacious and liked to spend money. It didn't matter whose money she spent.

It's a widely held belief that Virginia and Bugsy were stealing from his bosses in order to finance their lavish lifestyle, and this is the real reason that Bugsy was killed. The thefts might not have been so bad, had the Flamingo made money early on. But luck was against Bugsy on opening night December 1946.

Finally, at a cost of over five million dollars the Flamingo was open. It was wintertime in Las Vegas. A freak storm had hit the West Coast in full force. As heavy wind driven rain washed across the valley, Jimmy Durante, Rose Marie and other top name entertainers attempted to please the sparse crowd of gamblers who'd braved the elements to come out and see what the Flamingo was all about.

Notably absent was the western cowpoke look of the other Las Vegas establishments. The décor was modern up to the minute swank; class as interpreted by Benjamin Siegel. No bolo ties, boots or plaid shirts. Bugsy and staff were attired in formal wear. This probably seemed pretentious to those who were accustomed to the El Rancho Vegas and its heavy western theme. No one dared voice such an opinion as Bugsy greeted his guests warmly.

The hotel was still not complete, so as they grew weary of gambling, the customers had little choice but to leave the premises, taking their money with them. Three hundred miles away in Los Angeles would be patrons were kept away because the raging winter storm had grounded all planes. This was not at all what Bugsy had envisioned. Eventually he would be proven right; the Flamingo would become a huge money making success. Unfortunately Bugsy wouldn't be around to see it. On this night his bosses were furious with him. They'd squandered enough money in the Nevada desert. Now Siegel was on a crash course with destiny. No one could save him, not even his childhood friend Meyer Lansky.

The end came for Bugsy on June 20, 1947. In Las Vegas he'd been safe and protected. His penthouse at the Flamingo was locked behind a steel reinforced door, the windows were bullet proof, and in the closet was a special secret ladder escape that would take him to an awaiting getaway car in the garage tunnel that could lead him to safety in the eventuality...

Tonight Bugsy was staying at 810 Linden Street, Virginia Hill's rented Beverly Hills home. Virginia was away in Europe.

Bugsy and his friend had returned from their early dinner and settled onto the sofa. He switched on a reading lamp.

The killers had waited for the cover of darkness. Now it was time. This job would require stealth and cunning. Outside the window, they stopped and looked in at Siegel who glanced at the newspaper. They took aim...Three shots rang out in quick succession...Bugsy was no more. A shattered bloody corpse slumped on the colorful chintz sofa.

All that money and legalized gambling was just too good to pass up. The Flamingo would continue on.   Naturally there would be a change of management that would rush in to take care of the mob's hotel/casino. And as gamblers happily tossed money into the Flamingo's coffers, five mourners gathered to honor Benjamin (Bugsy) Siegel.

Tony Cornero Checks Out

People have wondered about Tony Cornero's *convenient* death since he dropped to the casino floor Sunday July 31, 1955. It could have been a heart attack. But was it? Tony Cornero died deeply in debt. A previous failed attempt on his life had given Tony a sense of security. It shouldn't have.

Tony was in Vegas and the proud owner of the all new Stardust Hotel. But Cornero didn't have the money to open the hotel. He'd gone through six million dollars of the mob's money and here he was begging for another $800,000. How else was he going to fill the cage with cash, and pay the food and liquor suppliers?

He left the decision makers to figure it out and headed for the craps table. He was a gambler. His luck would change. He was down $37,000. Sweating it out with each roll of the dice, Cornero started cursing the croupier, while the blonde hanging onto him tried to sweet talk him out of his tantrum. Winner or loser, drinks are on the house to players. But not today, a cocktail waitress showed up with a bill for Tony in the amount of $25.00 for the food and drink that he'd consumed.

It didn't get much more disrespectful than that. Tony was furious and loud. He was a player here and players are accorded perks. A cocktail waitress came along with a tray and a freebie drink for him. He took it and downed it.

Grabbing his chest, Tony Cornero dropped to the floor dead. His body was whisked to a private room where four hours would pass before the coroner was notified. Why the delay? Had Tony been poisoned? One thing we know, the glass from which the mobster drank was whisked away and washed clean. No germs and no evidence remained. An autopsy was not performed on Cornero. The coroner's jury found coronary thrombosis as the cause of death. And off to Los Angeles the dead Tony went for burial.

Timing is everything. Natural or not, Cornero's death was fortuitous for new owners and their management team at the Stardust.

Bye-Bye Fat Herbie

There was an unwritten rule in Las Vegas. And mobsters, for the most part, obeyed. Bugsy Siegel, Gus Greenbaum and Tony Spilotro knew that when it was time for a mobster to go, the deed was done elsewhere. No one wanted mobsters killing each other within the city limits. This brought a lot of heat and scared the tourists which was very bad for business.

There have been some exceptions. Fat Herbie Blitzstein's murder was one. In 1997 Blitzstein was a sick old man with a bad heart who made his living selling used cars. His days of guarding Tony Spilotro were long gone. Any power he may have held as a feared mob enforcer was also a thing of the past. Unfortunately for Herbie he had *friends* who wanted him gone as well. They struck a deal.

And on January 6, 1997 Fat Herbie walked into his Las Vegas townhome and found two men waiting for him. He realized this was it, the end of the road for him. One of the men pointed his pistol and took aim…

It's Not Smart to Rob the Mob

There is no luck worse than what the two men in this story faced. The story begins in Las Vegas and reaches its bloody conclusion in Los Angeles.

They were known as the *Two Tonys*, Tony Brancato and Tony Trombino two small time Kansas City crooks who worked in Los Angeles in the early 1940s. Besides dealing drugs and committing robberies Brancato did freelance hits for the mob. He was considered a suspect in the 1947 Beverly Hills slaying of mobster Bugsy Siegel. Live by the bullet, die by the bullet, Brancato would come to understand those words very well.

In 1951 the two Tonys came up with a surefire scheme. They would rob the sports book of the Flamingo Hotel in Las Vegas. Yes, that's the same Flamingo that was owned and operated by the mob.

The reckless duo cased the place and determined their plan foolproof. Only it wasn't. On May 28, 1951 the two Tonys went to the sportsbook and robbed it of $3500 which was a lot of money back in 1951. Instead of masks, the men wore hats to shield their identity from witnesses. But Lady Luck was elsewhere this day and Brancato's hat slipped. The sportsbook manager recognized him right away. Not only did Brancato end up on the FBI's most wanted list, he and Trombino ended up in the crosshairs of the mob. Brancato was arrested in San Francisco, posted the $10,000 bail and walked free. The FBI would have been a safer bet.

The mob was watching as Brancato and Trombino cheated their way around Los Angeles. The two Tonys stooped so low as to cheat another mobster at of several thousand dollars. Enough is enough. Gus Greenbaum, who would himself end up on the wrong side of a mob hit, ordered a hit on the two Tonys.

Jimmy Fratianno was told to do the deed. He laid out a scheme in which suggested the three of them could make a nice profit by robbing a high stakes poker game. Always hurting for cash, the two Tonys fell for it, and readily agreed.

August 6, 1951 a nice warm night in LA, it was about to get a whole lot hotter.

With Brancato in the front passenger seat, Trombino pulled the car up to the curb at 1648 N. Ogden Street in Hollywood, cut the engine and waited. Jimmy Fratianno jumped in the backseat of Trombino's car. Before Brancato could ask, "So where's this card game?"

Fratianno pulled his gun and unloaded it into the two Tony's brains.

The murders would remain unsolved until 1978 when Fratianno turned against his mob cronies and told it all. Afterwards he went into witness protection and lived to the ripe old age of eighty.

The Unsolved Mystery of Roy Frisch

In a 2016 article in the Nevada Appeal, Nevada historian/author Rich Moreno called Roy Frisch's disappearance Reno's *most puzzling mystery*.

Indeed it is. And every year on the anniversary of his disappearance, Roy Frisch is remembered in Reno with yet another theory as to what may have happened to him on the night of March 22, 1934.

One thing we do know, Frisch made a serious mistake. His fate was sealed when he talked to the grand jury, and agreed to testify in federal court against his bosses William Graham and James McKay. Graham and McKay ran Reno's underworld, and were up to their necks in all things illegal. They were also associated with George Wingfield, who at that time was Nevada's most powerful, make that wealthiest, man. How much did Wingfield know and when did he know it?

The feds were curious. Was the money from Graham's and McKay's illegal enterprises being laundered through George Wingfield's Riverside Bank where Roy Frisch worked as a cashier?

When he didn't return home the next day or the next, the family raised the alarm. Where was Roy? A large reward was offered. Searches were conducted. But no sign of Roy Frisch ever turned up.

Notorious bank robber Lester Gillis AKA Baby Face Nelson was in Reno at the time with his cohort John Paul Chase. Nelson was working as a bouncer, bodyguard and chauffeur for William Graham. It's probably no coincidence that Nelson and Chase headed to Illinois shortly after Frisch disappeared.

Fate caught up with Baby Face later that same year. He was killed on November 27, 1934 when FBI agents trapped him and Chase outside of Chicago and opened fire.

Although he managed to escape, Chase was later captured and charged with the murder of an FBI agent. Convicted, he was sentenced to life at Alcatraz.

A year after Frisch's disappearance the July 13, 1935 issue of the Reno Gazette Journal carried a story about John Paul Chase's confession of the crime. According to Chase, he and Nelson had encountered Frisch crossing the street and almost ran over him. A fight ensued; Nelson pistol whipped Frisch and threw him into their automobile where he was shot and killed. They then drove the body through Virginia City and onward south for a hundred miles before tossing it into a mineshaft. But, he couldn't remember where exactly that was.

Although, they didn't believe the entire story, the FBI closed the case on Roy Frisch's whereabouts. The rumors continue to this day. Some believe that Roy Frisch was buried in the backyard of George Wingfield's mansion which incidentally was located right next to the Frisch family home near downtown Reno.

In 1996 Reno Police reopened the case. Someone wanted to use ground penetrating radar to see if a body was indeed on the old Wingfield property. The owner refused to let them do so.

And the theories keep coming. Some have suggested that Frisch stole a pile of money from the bank and fled to sunny climes. He was very close with his mother and his sisters and this seems highly unlikely. And yet, no one probably saw D.B. Cooper as a hijacker until he actually leapt out of that plane.

Meanwhile, we ask ourselves, where is Roy Frisch?

Who Put the Hit on Barbara McNair's Husband?

It's a cold case, likely never to be solved. The 1976 murder of Rick Manzie in

his and his wife Barbara McNair's 20 room Las Vegas mansion had all the earmarks of be a hit, but who did it...and why?

It was believed that Manzie had mob connections. Tony Spilotro, who himself would end up the wrong end of a mob hit, was a good friend of Manzie. And he made it known that he wanted the killer of his friend found and dealt with. Well, that's one story anyway. But in his book *Rise and Fall of a Casino Mobster* Frank Cullotta tells a very different story. He claims that Spilotro was responsible for the murder because Manzie was abusive to McNair who Spilotro was having an affair with.

Barbara McNair was a beautiful African American singer and actress who built a substantial career for herself in a time when opportunity was scarce for people of color. In addition to her roles in movies and Broadway, she also had her own syndicated television show.

In 1972 at the height of her career, she married her manager Rick Manzie, a heroin addict with ties to some very dangerous people. The couple made Las Vegas their home by purchasing a 20 room mansion on Bruce Street near the Sahara Hotel

On December 16, 1976 while Barbara McNair was performing at a nightclub in Chicago, someone came into her home and shot her husband to death.

Like so many other mob hits, the killer (or killers) was never brought to justice.

Tony

Short and stocky Anthony Spilotro strutted into Vegas ready to strong arm anyone who got in the way of his and his bosses plans. Like Bugsy before him, Spilotro was a mobster. And like Bugsy, when he became a liability to his bosses, Spilotro was ushered from the Las Vegas scene, miles away.

The similarities end there. Where Siegel was handsome and debonair; Spilotro was anything but. The Las Vegas of the 1970's was very different from the Las Vegas of today. Mob enforcer, Spilotro had the juice. And was making piles of money. Then he went and pissed the wrong people off. Those into hauntings believe the ghostly Spilotro is keeping a low profile. Then again, perhaps his apparition still wanders through that Indiana cornfield trying to figure out how he went wrong.

Strange as it seems, some Las Vegans that worked in the service industry remember him as being kindhearted. Said a waitress, who waited on him several times at a hotel/casino that has long since been imploded,

"He was always so nice to me...always left me a good toke. When he was with a group of people who had finished their meal, he would ask them, 'What about the girl? Did you leave her a tip?' If they didn't answer him, he'd asked me, 'Honey did they get you?'

I knew who he was. Everyone did. And I knew who they were. So I just smiled and said, 'Yes sir. '

Another person, who wasn't impressed with Spilotro's generosity laughed, "Obviously good tokes don't mean jack when it comes to getting whacked in a cornfield. "

Obviously not!

Recently Spilotro's old digs in Las Vegas went up for sale. An ordinary house in an ordinary neighborhood, the 2400 square foot house located at 4675 Balfour Drive was offered at $420,000. Like most houses in Las Vegas, there's a pool in the backyard. A rather large pool. The thing is, Tony Spilotro lived here and ate here and slept here and made plans here...

The house sold fast. It didn't even stay on the market a month. Which begs the question; if he could talk what would Tony Spilotro say about all the interest?

ABOUT THE AUTHOR

Janice Oberding is the author of several other books including Haunted Virginia City, Haunted Reno, Haunted Lake Tahoe, The Ghosts and Legends of Goldfield and Tonopah, The Boy Nevada Killed, A Death in Tonopah, Abracadaver, Demon Song and Tiptoe Through the Tombstones. When not writing she enjoys reading, antiquing, trying new recipes, and traveling with family and friends, especially her husband Bill, who also serves as photographer.

50292458R00059

Made in the USA
Columbia, SC
06 February 2019